BEER HIKING
NEW YORK STATE

THE TASTIEST WAY TO DISCOVER THE EMPIRE STATE

Beer Hiking New York State
The Tastiest Way to Discover the Empire State

By: Jason Friedman and Philip Vondra

ISBN: 978-3-0396-4021-8
Published by Helvetiq, Lausanne/Basel, Switzerland
Cover design: Ajša Zdravković
Graphic design and illustration: Daniel Malak, Jędrzej Malak (maps)
Photography: See page 224 for photo credits
Printed in the United Kingdom
First edition: September 2023

Copyright © 2023 Helvetiq, Switzerland
info@helvetiq.ch

www.helvetiq.com/us
www.facebook.com/helvetiq.usa
instagram: @helvetiq_usa

helvetiq.com

BEER HIKING NEW YORK STATE

THE TASTIEST WAY TO DISCOVER THE EMPIRE STATE

TABLE OF CONTENTS

1

INTRODUCTION

ABOUT THE AUTHORS

Jason Friedman and Phil Vondra have been running partners, hiking buddies, and fellow beer enthusiasts since meeting on a trail run in New Paltz, NY, in the early aughts. Since then, they've run and hiked thousands of miles and sampled hundreds of brews together. They are the co-hosts of the popular podcast *The Pain Cave,* which focuses on trail running, ultrarunning, and beer.

Jason is an emergency-medicine and sports-medicine physician and exercise physiologist who coaches marathon and ultramarathon runners for Boundless Endurance Coaching. A lifelong runner, he has completed over fifty ultramarathons and is a former age-group national champion at 100 kilometers. He is a member of the Catskill 3500 club, having summitted all 33 Catskill peaks over 3,500 feet. Jason's writing has appeared in *Ultrarunning* and *Marathon and Beyond* magazines, and his blog, *A Muddy Pair of Heels,* was a two-time finalist for RunUltra's Blog of the Year. He enjoys scenic hikes over runnable terrain and is partial to farmhouse ales and sours.

Philip is a former rock climber and a world-class rower who was once an alternate for the British Olympic team. After moving to New Paltz, he took his love of the outdoors to the trails, becoming a prolific hiker and ultramarathoner. He has completed over thirty ultras and is a five-time age-group national champion. He is a member of the Catskill 3500 club and is also an Adirondack "46er" having summitted the forty-six highest peaks in the state's largest park. He currently holds records for the fastest summitting of all the Catskill high peaks in winter—a feat he accomplished in less than 3.5 days—and is the only person to have completed a "Grid"—hiking every summit in every month of the year—over a consecutive 12-month span. He likes scrambling over steep, technical terrain and prefers IPAs and barrel-aged stouts.

ABOUT BEER HIKING IN NEW YORK

One would be hard-pressed to find a better place to combine the twin passions of hiking and beer than the state of New York. With over 450 craft breweries, New York trails only California in number of breweries, and its 215 state parks also rank second to the Golden State.

As a hiking destination, New York defies categorization. The running joke is that everything north of New York City is referred to as "Upstate." But to paint with such a broad brush neglects the natural variation that makes exploring the outdoors in New York such a fulfilling experience. From the fertile farmlands of the Hudson River Valley, where the maple trees explode into mind-bending color palettes each fall, to the ancient, mysterious forests of the Catskill Mountains, to the majestic beauty and cascading waterfalls of the Finger Lakes, to the wild High Peaks of the Adirondacks—there's a hike for everyone in New York. We've tried to get a little of the flavor of all these areas into this book, and also to explore some of the rich history of our great state, which has played such a pivotal role in shaping this country.

A sense of community and environmental stewardship pervades New York hiking culture. Groups like the Catskill 3500 Club and the Adirondack 46ers, made up of hikers who summit the highest peaks in each of these classic regions, help to build this culture by educating members and the general public on responsible land use and safe outdoor recreation, and adopt trails for maintenance and upkeep. The New York-New Jersey Trail Conference is another volunteer organization dedicated to conservation and sustainability that builds and maintains trails and provides resources to hikers throughout the region.

The union of hiking and beer is a logical pairing. Both outdoor enthusiasts and craft brewers share a concern for preserving the local environment. The art of craft brewing relies on utilizing the natural resources of the area—its water, soil, and agriculture—to impart distinctive character to the product. New York's Empire State Development office has been committed to supporting the craft beverage industry, incentivizing brewers to use locally sourced ingredients and keeping the state on the cutting edge of craft brewing.

Though the scope of this guide is limited to day hikes, New York boasts a plethora of experiences for the thru-hiker. The 350-mile Long Path starts across the George Washington Bridge from Manhattan and extends north to Albany. The Finger Lakes Trail stretches 580 rugged miles from the western Pennsylvania border east into the Catskill Mountains. The 138-mile Northville-Placid Trail, one of the oldest hiking paths in the country, traverses much of the Adirondacks. And connecting many of these regions is the 750-mile Empire State Trail, the longest multi-use trail in the United States. Several of the hikes in this guide intersect with these and other classic long hikes, and we hope that this serves as inspiration for intrepid hikers to tackle some of these longer routes.

CHOOSE THE BEER OR THE HIKE

HIKE LOCATION ⟶

REGION ⟶

MAP ⟶

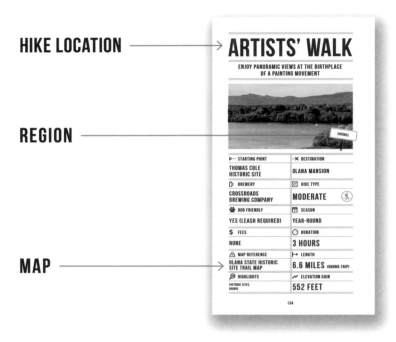

ARTISTS' WALK

ENJOY PANORAMIC VIEWS AT THE BIRTHPLACE OF A PAINTING MOVEMENT

CATSKILL

▷— STARTING POINT	—✕ DESTINATION
THOMAS COLE HISTORIC SITE	OLANA MANSION
⌂ BREWERY	HIKE TYPE
CROSSROADS BREWING COMPANY	MODERATE
DOG FRIENDLY	SEASON
YES (LEASH REQUIRED)	YEAR-ROUND
$ FEES	⏱ DURATION
NONE	3 HOURS
MAP REFERENCE	↦ LENGTH
OLANA STATE HISTORIC SITE TRAIL MAP	6.6 MILES (ROUND-TRIP)
HIGHLIGHTS	ELEVATION GAIN
HISTORIC SITES, BRIDGE	552 FEET

134

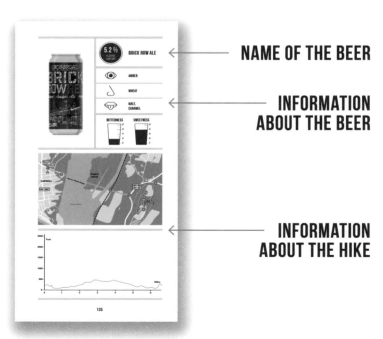

5.2 % ALCOHOL CONTENT — BRICK ROW ALE ⟵ **NAME OF THE BEER**

👁 AMBER

👃 WHEAT

👅 MALT, CARAMEL ⟵ **INFORMATION ABOUT THE BEER**

BITTERNESS   SWEETNESS

⟵ **INFORMATION ABOUT THE HIKE**

135

ON THE HIKES AND HIKE RATINGS

The hikes in this book are classified into three categories of overall difficulty. We've tried to take into account distance, elevation gain, and terrain when rating these routes. These classifications are by nature subjective; what we feel is a moderate hike might be considered strenuous (or easy!) by someone else. Please note also that difficulty is subject to trail conditions, as heavy rain, snow, leaf cover, and blowdown can all make a hike more challenging than it would be in clear, dry conditions.

 Easy trails are generally on the shorter end of the spectrum, though there are a couple of longer routes that we've rated as "easy" owing to their minimal elevation gain and ease of use. Most of these trails are relatively wide and flat, and all feature non-technical footing that is simple to navigate. These routes are often suitable for trail running or cycling as well.

 Moderate trails comprise the majority of hikes in this book. These routes generally present more of a challenge, usually involving narrower trails with more elevation gain, but rarely steep pitches or highly technical terrain. Experienced trail runners or mountain bikers may feel comfortable tackling these trails in those disciplines, though this should be approached with caution.

 Strenuous trails involve a good bit of climbing—at least 200 feet of elevation gain per mile on average, and in some cases significantly more than that. In addition, many of these trails are narrow, rocky, and quite technical. While we don't consider any of these routes dangerous—none of them involve any high-angle exposure, nor do they require any climbing gear or mountaineering expertise—hikers attempting these trails should have at least a modicum of previous outdoor experience. Be prepared for longer days with more unpredictable conditions, not just in terms of footing but also with regard to weather and daylight.

Hikes are further classified by type. A loop is a continuous path that begins and ends at the same point, with a minimum of backtracking or retracing of steps. A round-trip route, also termed an out-and-back, turns around at its destination and follows the same route back to the finish. A lollipop is a combination of the two: it involves hiking to a specific point, making a loop that returns to that point, and then returning to the start via the initial path. The few point-to-point hikes in this book end in a different spot than they began; in these cases, we've included instructions on how to get back to the trailhead.

Many of the hikes in this book explore New York's numerous state parks, most of which charge an entry fee to park and use their facilities. If you're planning on enjoying these parks, consider purchasing an Empire Pass, which provides you (and anyone else in your car) unlimited access to all of New York's state parks. As we write this, annual passes are $80, and multi-year and lifetime passes are also available.

ON THE BREWERIES AND BEER RATINGS

New York has a rich tradition of brewing and has had an outsized influence on the craft brewing revolution of the past few decades. In our brewery and beer choices, we aim to recognize and pay homage to that tradition, while also highlighting some of the exciting brewers and brands pushing the boundaries of modern beermaking. As with many other East Coast brewing regions, New York yielded a profusion of hoppy American ales and IPAs in the early stages of the craft beer movement. Over the past several years, an emphasis on farm licensing and local agriculture has contributed to an explosion of farmhouse ales, saisons, and sours. We've tried to include a wide variety of styles among our featured beers. In many cases, we've highlighted the flagship beer for a particular brewery, but by no means are these the only beers worth trying. In most cases, the highlighted beers should be available year-round, but seasonal and experimental offerings add exciting variety to the lineups in most tasting rooms and we encourage you to branch out and experience as many different styles and flavors as you can.

Each section includes notes on a particular beer's color, aroma, taste, bitterness, and sweetness. These notes are arguably even more subjective than the ratings for the hikes; one person's perception of bitterness, or ability to pick out subtle undertones in taste or aroma, may not be the same as another's. None of these ratings should be considered definitive, but we hope they will serve as a useful starting point when exploring New York's craft beers.

It should go without saying that being responsible while beer hiking is an absolute must. There's a reason the hikes are listed before the breweries—that's the order in which they should be enjoyed. While a beer on-trail can be a refreshing treat, you should NEVER hike while intoxicated. And of course, under no circumstances should you drink and drive.

The breweries selected for this book were chosen for several reasons: proximity to hikes we enjoyed, reputation, recommendations by other beer enthusiasts, and our own experience. We've tried to include both well-known brands and some that might be less familiar. For the most part, we've focused on breweries rather than brewpubs; when visiting the latter, we favor restaurants that place a high priority on the brewing process and product. With over 450 breweries in the state, chances are that your favorite was omitted. Sorry! It's a numbers game. If enough of you clamor for our wonderful publisher to produce a second edition, we'll do our utmost to include it next time.

PREPARING FOR YOUR HIKE

TEN ESSENTIALS (AND ONE MORE)

There is no surer way to turn an amazing day on the trails into an unpleasant (and possibly dangerous) experience than to start a hike unprepared. Even if you're only heading out for a short hike, expect and plan for the unexpected, and include these essentials in your pack.

- Navigation: Even in areas with well-marked trails, you should always carry a map. The maps in this book, while helpful, should be used for reference purposes only. Many websites have downloadable maps, and GPS files can be easily accessed on your phone. However, never rely solely on your phone's battery. Carry a topographical map of the region and a compass and know how to use them.
- First aid kit: You can find premade backcountry kits at most outdoor supply stores or build your own.
- Hydration: Even water sources marked on maps may be unreliable. Carry enough water to last for the entirety of your planned hike and have at least one method of filtration/purification with you, such as a water filter or UV purifier. Consider bringing iodine tablets as a backup in case your primary method malfunctions.
- Nutrition: Bring enough food to fuel your exertions on the trail, but also pack some extra, calorie-dense foods that can sustain you if you're out for longer than expected.
- Sun protection: A hat with a brim, sunglasses, and sunscreen all help shield you from glare and sunburn. Don't neglect this in the winter, when reflected light off snow can intensify the effects of sunlight on unprotected skin.
- Extra clothing: Weather can change quickly, especially in the mountains. Don't get caught in a storm without good rain gear. Also, bring at least one extra layer of warm clothing, as temperatures can plummet once the sun begins to set.
- Hardware: A small kit consisting of a pocketknife or multi-tool, a length of twine or rope, and a roll of duct tape can be useful in any number of situations in the wilderness, from first aid to building shelter to repairing gear.
- Light: A headlamp or flashlight can be a literal lifesaver when trying to navigate after dark. Make sure to check the batteries before you leave and keep extra batteries in your pack.
- Fire starter: In an emergency, the ability to start a fire for warmth can be lifesaving. Keep waterproof matches in a waterproof container in your pack.
- Shelter: A lightweight tent is essential when hiking in the backcountry, but even a space blanket can serve as an emergency shelter if necessary.
- Satellite beacon: There are several small, light GPS locators on the market that can monitor your position and alert rescuers in case of emergency.

HIKING SEASON

Each season brings its own rewards and challenges for hikers. Spring and autumn are generally prime hiking times, and the peak time for fall foliage—from late September through early November—is particularly beautiful. Spring can often bring muddy trails, so wear waterproof shoes with good traction. Late spring and early summer are blackfly season in the Adirondacks; wear bug spray or stay indoors and avoid these bloodsuckers. Drink plenty of water and guard against heat exposure in the summer. Hiking in the winter can be particularly gratifying, but often requires extra gear and accessories, including crampons or snowshoes to provide traction and break trail in icy or snowy conditions.

HUNTING SEASON

Hunting is permitted in most state parks and on lands managed by the Department of Environmental Conservation. Depending on region, method, and quarry, the season can extend from mid-September through late January. Always wear bright, blaze-orange clothing when hiking during this period, and be aware of the local hunting laws and seasons, which can be found on the DEC website (www.dec.ny.gov/outdoor/hunting.html).

WEATHER

There's an expression favored by hikers in the Catskills and Adirondacks: "If you don't like the weather, wait five minutes." To paraphrase Heraclitus, when it comes to hiking weather in New York, the only constant is change. Be prepared for all possibilities when setting out on a hike, particularly in the mountains, where conditions at higher elevations may differ drastically from those at the trailhead. The National Weather Service website (www.weather.gov) and Mountain Weather Forecasts (www.mountain-forecast.com) can be especially helpful when planning your trip.

ADDITIONAL RESOURCES

HIKING

www.catskill-3500-club.org
www.adk46er.org
www.nynjtc.org
www.alltrails.com
www.dec.ny.gov
www.parks.ny.gov

BREWERIES

www.tap-ny.com
www.newyorkcraftbeer.com
www.iloveny.com/things-to-do/food/breweries/
www.nycbrewed.com
www.governor.ny.gov/sites/default/files/atoms/files/400_NYS_Breweries.pdf

VISITOR AMENITIES

www.iloveny.com
www.esd.gov.ny
www.discoverupstateny.com
www.nystia.org

TRAIL ETIQUETTE

Hiking around our great state presents wonderful opportunities, but it is also a privilege. When adventuring outdoors, we should all take it upon ourselves to be good trail citizens, showing respect for the land, its stewards, and our fellow hikers. As a general guideline, practice the Golden Rule: treat others as you would wish to be treated, and by extension, treat the shared environment as you would treat your own private environment.

Some more specific principles:

- Know and obey the rules and regulations set by the land managers of the area you'll be visiting.
- When possible, plan to visit in small groups during times of lower trail usage to minimize the impact on the environment.
- Be considerate of other hikers and trail users. Yield to uphill hikers and horseback riders, who have the right-of-way. Refrain from playing loud music, which not only disturbs other hikers and wildlife, but makes it more difficult to stay aware of your own surroundings.
- Practice Leave No Trace principles. Travel on established trails; don't cut switchbacks or otherwise trample off-trail vegetation. Dispose of waste properly. Don't disturb or transport natural objects, vegetation, or historic structures or artifacts. Learn more about the Leave No Trace movement for Outdoor Ethics at www.lnt.org.
- Respect wildlife. Observe fauna from a distance; do not follow or approach animals. NEVER feed wildlife, as it can alter their natural behavior and create dangerous environments and interactions as well as have a negative impact on their health.

Like many other hikers, we love spending time on the trail with our dogs. In fact, Phil's labradoodle, George, is himself a member of the Catskill 3500 club. If you're going hiking with your furry trail companion, all of the above recommendations are doubly applicable. Obey all local laws and regulations, including leash laws—we're not aware of any dog-friendly hikes that allow pets to be off-leash. Remember that while you love your pup, not all trail users will; make sure your animal is under your control at all times and respect the preferences of those around you. Even in the wilderness, clean up after your pets, as their waste may introduce artificial elements that can disturb the local ecosystem. And no, "cleaning up" does not mean leaving bags of dog poop on the side of the trail for park rangers to remove, or for you to come back and pick up later. Finally, be sure to check your pup—and yourself—for ticks following every hike, as Lyme disease and other tick-borne illnesses have become increasingly prevalent throughout New York State.

2

MAP & INDEX

MAP

401   **Kingston**

Lake Ontario

onto

Lake Erie

90

30   390

33

31   32

86

PA

180

80

80

99

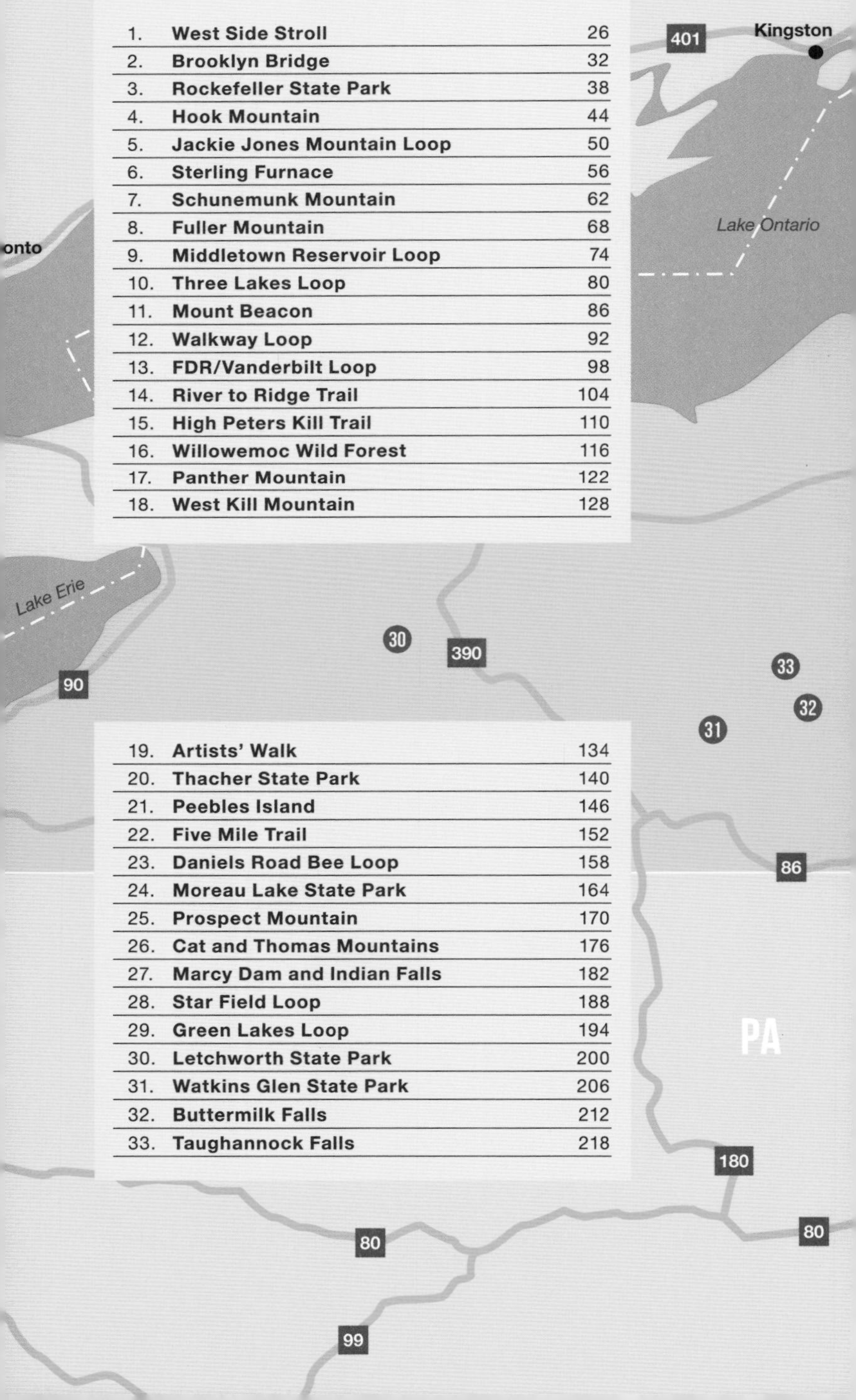

HIKES

NAME OF THE ROUTE	TOWN, PROVINCE, OR PARK	LENGTH	PAGE
Artists' Walk	Catskill	6.6 miles (round-trip)	134
Brooklyn Bridge	Brooklyn	4.5 miles (point-to-point)	32
Buttermilk Falls	Ithaca	4.6 miles (loop)	212
Cat and Thomas Mountains	Bolton Landing	7.2 miles (lollipop)	176
Daniels Road Bee Loop	Saratoga Springs	3.7 miles (lollipop)	158
FDR/Vanderbilt Loop	Hyde Park	9.0 miles (lollipop)	98
Five Mile Trail	Saratoga Springs	5.2 miles (loop)	152
Fuller Mountain	Warwick	2.6 miles (round-trip)	68
Green Lakes Loop	Manlius	2.9 miles (loop)	194
High Peters Kill Trail	Gardiner	4.4 miles (loop)	110
Hook Mountain	Nyack	6.1 miles (loop)	44
Jackie Jones Mountain Loop	Stony Point	4.1 miles (loop)	50
Letchworth State Park	Castile	10.1 miles (round-trip)	200
Marcy Dam and Indian Falls	Lake Placid	9.9 miles (lollipop)	182
Middletown Reservoir Loop	Middletown	6.9 miles (lollipop)	74
Moreau Lake State Park	Gansevoort	4.3 miles (loop)	164
Mount Beacon	Beacon	3.9 miles (round-trip)	86
Panther Mountain	Phoenicia	6.5 miles (round-trip)	122
Peebles Island	Cohoes	2.0 miles (loop)	146
Prospect Mountain	Lake George	3.1 miles (round-trip)	170
River to Ridge Trail	New Paltz	7.6 miles (round-trip)	104
Rockefeller State Park	Pleasantville	6.2 miles (loop)	38
Schunemunk Mountain	Cornwall	7.4 miles (loop)	62
Star Field Loop	Cooperstown	4.2 miles (lollipop)	188
Sterling Furnace	Tuxedo	3.9 miles (loop)	56
Taughannock Falls	Trumansburg	2.0 miles (round-trip)	218
Thacher State Park	Voorheesville	4.1 miles (loop)	140
Three Lakes Loop	Putnam Valley	3.6 miles (loop)	80
Walkway Loop	Poughkeepsie	3.1 miles (point-to-point)	92
Watkins Glen State Park	Watkins Glen	2.4 miles (loop)	206
West Kill Mountain	West Kill	6.5 miles (round-trip)	128
West Side Stroll	Manhattan	4.2 miles (point-to-point)	26
Willowemoc Wild Forest	Livingston Manor	6.8 miles (loop)	116

BREWERIES & BEERS

BREWERY	BEER	PAGE
Adirondack Brewery	Bear Naked Ale	170
Artisanal Brew Works	Trappist at the Track Tripel	158
Bolton Landing Brewing Company	Morning Pitch blonde ale	176
Brewery Ommegang	Hennepin farmhouse saison	188
Buried Acorn Brewing Company	Ghoster Blanc sour	194
Bye-i Brewing	Midnight Veil stout	146
Captain Lawrence Brewing Company	Orbital Tilt IPA	38
Catskill Brewery	Nightshine black lager	116
Crossroads Brewing Company	Brick Row ale	134
Dancing Grain Farm Brewery	Harvest Sun saison	164
Druthers Brewing Company	Golden Rule blonde ale	152
Equilibrium Brewery	Photon pale ale	74
Foreign Objects Beer Company	Hanging Garden pale ale	56
Hudson Valley Brewery	Incandenza sour IPA	86
Indian Ladder Farms Cidery and Brewery	Indian Lager Farms	140
Industrial Arts Brewing Company	Wrench IPA	50
Ithaca Beer Company	Flower Power IPA	212
Lake Placid Pub & Brewery	Ubu Ale	182
Liquid State Brewing Company	Daypack Saison	218
Marlowe Artisanal Ales	Eager to Share pale ale	44
Mill House Brewing Company	Kold One Kolsch	98
Other Half Brewing Company	Green City IPA	32
Rough Cut Brewing Co.	Minnewaska Trail Pale Ale	110
Rushing Duck Brewery	Imperial Beanhead Porter	62
Silver Lake Brewing Project	The Standard cream ale	200
Sloop Brewing Company	Juice Bomb IPA	80
The Drowned Lands	Gather House witbier	68
Torch & Crown Brewing Company	Almost Famous IPA	26
Upstate Brewing Company	Common Sense ale	206
West Kill Brewing	Kaaterskill IPA	128
Woodstock Brewing	Baby Dragon pale ale	122
Yard Owl Craft Brewery	Grisette	104
Zeus Brewing Company	Urban Oasis sour	92

3

THE BEER HIKES

WEST SIDE STROLL

AN URBAN HIKE THROUGH THE HEART OF NYC

MANHATTAN

▷⋯ STARTING POINT	⋯✗ DESTINATION
PORT AUTHORITY BUS TERMINAL	**WEST SIDE DRIVE, HIGH LINE, LITTLE ISLAND**
🍺 BREWERY	卍 HIKE TYPE
TORCH & CROWN BREWING COMPANY	**EASY**
🐾 DOG FRIENDLY	SEASON
NO	**YEAR-ROUND**
$ FEES	⏱ DURATION
NONE	**1 HOUR 30 MIN.**
⛰ MAP REFERENCE	⊢ LENGTH
NEW YORK CITY STREET MAP	**4.2 MILES** (POINT-TO-POINT)
🔍 HIGHLIGHTS	〰 ELEVATION GAIN
URBAN PARKS, TOURIST ATTRACTIONS	**21 FEET**

6.6%

ALCOHOL
CONTENT

ALMOST FAMOUS IPA

HAZY GOLD

PEACH,
HOPS

PINEAPPLE,
CITRUS,
PINE

BITTERNESS

5
4
3
2
1

SWEETNESS

5
4
3
2
1

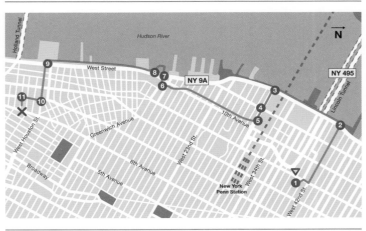

Hudson River

Holland Tunnel

West Street

NY 9A

NY 495

Lincoln Tunnel

10th Avenue

Greenwich Avenue

West Houston St.

West 23rd St.

West 34th St.

6th Avenue

5th Avenue

Broadway

New York
Penn Station

West 42nd St.

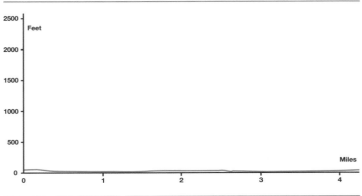

2500 — Feet
2000 —
1500 —
1000 —
500 —
0 —

Miles

0   1   2   3   4

HIKE DESCRIPTION

Tour some of the iconic sights, parks, and neighborhoods of the Big Apple before ending your hike at the only brewery on the island of Manhattan.

Manhattan isn't all skyscrapers and taxi cabs. With parks and pedestrian paths scattered throughout the island, New York City is a hidden hiker's paradise. There are countless options for visiting New York's innumerable attractions on foot. This tour of the Lower West Side links several parks and sights on the way to a brewery in one of the city's most famous neighborhoods.

The Port Authority Bus Terminal's central location and ease of access make it an ideal "trailhead" for west side walking. Easily reachable by bus or train, this midtown transportation hub is only steps from Times

Square and the theater district. Madison Square Garden, "The World's Most Famous Arena," is less than half a mile to the south; the Empire State Building is a fifteen-minute walk to the east. For this hike, you'll head west toward the Hudson River, where a pedestrian path parallels the West Side Highway. Looking north, you'll be able to see the USS Intrepid, a decommissioned World War II aircraft carrier that serves as the centerpiece of a fascinating military museum.

Sharing the path with runners and cyclists, head south for about half a mile, with the New Jersey city of Hoboken visible across the river on your right. Leave the path at 30th Street and climb a staircase to enter Hudson Yards, a self-contained neighborhood featuring open plazas. The centerpiece of this area is the Vessel, a massive structure of "interactive artwork" where visitors can climb between 154 interconnected flights of stairs to different vantage points over the city.

Leave Hudson Yards on the High Line, a public park built on an old elevated train line featuring gardens, viewpoints, and sculptures. The park ends at Chelsea Market, a bustling shopping destination in a neighborhood historically renowned for the arts and as a bastion of gay culture. One of the newest parks in Chelsea is Little Island, a two-acre oasis built on the remnants of an old pier. This community hub features striking architecture, landscaping, and gardens, along with an open-air amphitheater for live performances.

Heading south from Little Island, you'll pass Chelsea Piers, with views of the Freedom Tower at Ground Zero straight ahead, before entering SoHo, a former industrial area now known for its hip, bohemian, artsy vibe. The brewery is in this neighborhood, right next door to the Spring Street station, which allows you to make an easy return trip to the start via subway, or can serve as a launching point for further exploration of the world's greatest city.

TURN-BY-TURN DIRECTIONS

1. From Port Authority, head north on Ninth Avenue, then make an immediate left on 42nd Street and head west.
2. At 0.6 miles, cross the West Side Highway and make a left, heading south on the pedestrian path.
3. At 1.3 miles, turn left at 30th Street. Cross back over the West Side Highway and follow 30th Street east for one block.
4. At 1.5 miles, reach a staircase at the northwest corner of 30th Street and 11th Avenue. Climb the stairs. At the top, turn right, following the High Line east.
5. At 1.6 miles, pass the Vessel on the left. Follow the High Line as it turns right/south.
6. At 2.5 miles, pass Chelsea Market on the left. Descend the stairs to West 14th Street. At the base of the stairs, turn left and head west toward the Hudson River.
7. At 2.6 miles, continue straight to enter Little Island.
8. At 2.7 miles, exit Little Island and turn right, following the pedestrian path south along West Side Highway.
9. At 3.6 miles, turn left onto West Houston Street.
10. At 3.9 miles, turn right onto Varick Street.
11. At 4.1 miles, turn left onto Vandam Street. The brewery is one block east, on the right/south side of the street.

FIND THE TRAILHEAD

You can reach Port Authority by any number of bus routes, or by taking the A, C, E, N, Q, R, W, 1, 2, 3, or 7 trains. There is also a shuttle connecting Port Authority to Grand Central Station.

TORCH & CROWN BREWING COMPANY

Manhattan-dwelling beer aficionados tired of taking the train to sample Brooklyn's many breweries rejoiced upon the opening of Torch & Crown in 2020. The brewery's name pays homage to the iconography of the Statue of Liberty, which welcomes immigrants to the city. The brew tanks that stand amid the high top tables in the dining area each bear the name of a legendary New York rapper, underscoring the co-founders' love of the Beastie Boys and the Wu-Tang Clan. The beer list rotates seasonal varieties among the year-round favorites, and the kitchen offers shareable plates, burgers, and steaks. Downstairs, the Brewer's Cellar is available for private parties, as is the outdoor heated tent. If you haven't gotten your full hiking fix, the brewery offers walking tours of SoHo, which focus on the beer history of lower Manhattan before ending with lunch and beers.

LAND MANAGER

New York City Department of Parks and Recreation
The Arsenal, Central Park
830 Fifth Avenue
New York, NY 10065
(212) 639-9675
www.nycgovparks.org
Map: www.streets.planning.nyc.gov/about

BREWERY/RESTAURANT

Torch & Crown Brewing Company
12 Vandam Street
New York, NY 10013
(212) 228-7005
www.torchandcrown.com
Distance from trailhead: 4.2 miles

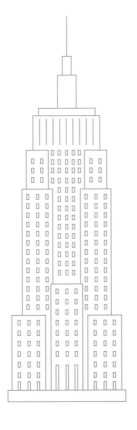

BROOKLYN BRIDGE

EXPERIENCE A HISTORIC NEW YORK LANDMARK

BROOKLYN

▷⋯ STARTING POINT	⋯✗ DESTINATION
NEW YORK CITY HALL	**BROOKLYN BRIDGE PARK**
🍺 BREWERY	HIKE TYPE
OTHER HALF BREWING COMPANY	**EASY**
🐾 DOG FRIENDLY	📅 SEASON
YES (LEASH REQUIRED)	**YEAR-ROUND**
$ FEES	🕐 DURATION
NONE	**1 HOUR 45 MIN.**
🗺 MAP REFERENCE	↦ LENGTH
BROOKLYN BRIDGE PARK MAP	**4.5 MILES** (POINT-TO-POINT)
🔍 HIGHLIGHTS	〜 ELEVATION GAIN
BRIDGE, RIVERFRONT	**212 FEET**

7.0% ALCOHOL CONTENT

GREEN CITY IPA

 HAZY YELLOW

CITRUS

TROPICAL FRUIT, ORANGE, GRASS

BITTERNESS

SWEETNESS

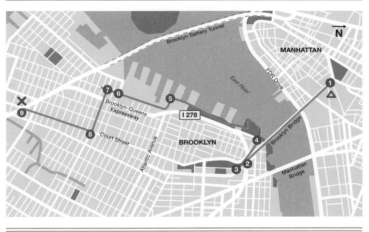

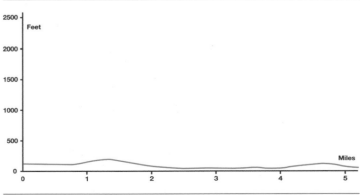

HIKE DESCRIPTION

Discover the reinvigorated borough of Brooklyn by crossing the famous Brooklyn Bridge and strolling down the East River to the neighborhood of Red Hook, where the hidden gem that is Other Half Brewing Company produces some of the best IPAs you'll ever taste.

The idea of "Brooklyn" may conjure up images of hot dogs on the Coney Island boardwalk and hipster dads in Prospect Park, but New Yorkers know that the borough as a whole resists categorization. If it were its own city, Brooklyn would be the fourth largest in the US, with over 2.7 million residents living in dozens of distinct neighborhoods, spread out over an area larger than Washington, D.C.

Among the many sights and attractions around New York City, few are as iconic as the Brooklyn Bridge. A wonder of 19th-century engineering, it took 13 years to complete, cost $15 million—over $300 million in today's dollars—and claimed the lives of 27 workers. Upon its completion in 1883, it was the longest suspension bridge in the world. It has

remained a crucial connection between Manhattan, Brooklyn, and the rest of Long Island, as well as an enduring tourist attraction. An estimated 100,000 cars and 10,000 pedestrians cross the bridge daily, and it sees over a million tourist visits a year.

Start your hike from City Hall on the Manhattan side of the bridge. This massive marble structure, built in 1812, is one of the oldest in the country to still serve its original governmental functions. Crossing southeast over Centre Street, you're just steps from the pedestrian promenade across the Brooklyn Bridge. It's impossible to cross this structure without marveling at the thousands of crisscrossing cables that help suspend the bridge deck above the East River, nearly 130 feet below. From the span, the views of Brooklyn, Queens, lower Manhattan, Governors Island, and the Statue of Liberty are magnificent.

After crossing the bridge, descend the stairs and make your way down to the East River to walk through Brooklyn Bridge Park, a 1.3-mile-long public space along the waterfront that features gardens, art installations, picnic facilities, piers, and athletic fields. You'll have nice views of the bridge and the Statue of Liberty as you head south along the water. After leaving the park, you'll pass through Cobble Hill before reaching Red Hook, a gentrifying neighborhood in an old shipping district bursting with restaurants and, of course, breweries.

TURN-BY-TURN DIRECTIONS

1.   Start from the City Hall/Brooklyn Bridge subway stop on Centre Street. Cross Centre Street to the south and follow signs for the Brooklyn Bridge. The pedestrian walkway over the bridge is directly ahead.
2.   At 1.1 miles, the pedestrian path forks. Bear left and descend a flight of stairs. At the bottom of the stairs, head left, then make an immediate left on Prospect Street.
3.   At 1.3 miles, turn right onto Old Fulton Street.
4.   At 1.5 miles, enter Brooklyn Bridge Park. Turn left, following the pedestrian path south along the river.
5.   At 2.8 miles, exit the park on Atlantic Avenue. Make an immediate right turn onto Columbia Street, following the shared bike/footpath.
6.   At 3.3 miles, the footpath turns right on Degraw Street. Continue straight on the Columbia Street sidewalk.
7.   At 3.4 miles, turn left on Union Street.
8.   At 3.9 miles, turn right on Court Street.
9.   At 4.5 miles, make a soft left on Hamilton Street, then an immediate left on Centre Street. The brewery is on the left.

FIND THE TRAILHEAD

New York City Hall has a dedicated subway station, making it easy to reach from almost anywhere in the city. Out-of-town visitors can take the train directly from the Port Authority Bus Terminal using the N, Q, R, and W lines, or take the 4, 5, or 6 train from Grand Central Station.

OTHER HALF BREWING COMPANY

Unlike the relative beer desert of Manhattan to the northwest, Brooklyn is absolutely teeming with breweries. Brooklyn Brewery in Williamsburg was one of the early pioneers of the craft beer movement; Threes, Evil Twin, and Sixpoint are all well-known breweries with widespread regional distribution. But few of these can match the fervor that greets new releases at Other Half Brewing Company, where a fresh style or limited-edition variety will have local beer aficionados literally lined up around the block. The tasting room is small and sparse, and the food options are limited to a few bags of chips, but the brews, particularly the IPAs and stouts, are second to none. There are twenty taps in the tasting room with a rotating selection of experimental varieties. Since the brewery opened in 2014, its brand has grown rapidly; there are satellite brewhouses and tasting rooms throughout the city, in upstate New York, and as far south as Philadelphia and Washington, D.C. The Smith-9th Street subway station is two blocks away; you can take the F or G train back toward Manhattan and change for any line running to City Hall.

LAND MANAGER

New York City Parks Department
The Arsenal, Central Park
830 Fifth Avenue
New York, NY 10065
(888) 697-2757
www.nycgovparks.org
Map: www.brooklynbridgepark.org/map

BREWERY/RESTAURANT

Other Half Brewing Company
195 Centre Street
Brooklyn, NY 11231
(212) 564-6065
www.otherhalfbrewing.com
Distance from trailhead: 4.5 miles

ROCKEFELLER STATE PARK

TOUR CARRIAGE ROADS ALONG WOODED STREAMS AND PASTURES

PLEASANTVILLE

▷··· STARTING POINT	···✕ DESTINATION
ROCKEFELLER STATE PARK PRESERVE VISITOR CENTER	**GLACIAL ERRATIC AND SWAN LAKE**
🍺 BREWERY	HIKE TYPE
CAPTAIN LAWRENCE BREWING COMPANY	**EASY**
🐾 DOG FRIENDLY	SEASON
YES (LEASH REQUIRED)	**YEAR-ROUND**
$ FEES	⏱ DURATION
$6 (FREE WITH EMPIRE PASS)	**2 HOURS 30 MIN.**
⌂ MAP REFERENCE	↦ LENGTH
POSTED AT TRAILHEAD	**6.2 MILES** (LOOP)
🔍 HIGHLIGHTS	∿ ELEVATION GAIN
GEOLOGIC FORMATION, STREAMS, LAKE	**410 FEET**

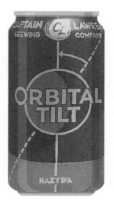

ORBITAL TILT IPA

HAZY ORANGE

CITRUS

CITRUS,
HOP BITE

BITTERNESS	SWEETNESS
5	5
4	4
3	3
2	2
1	1

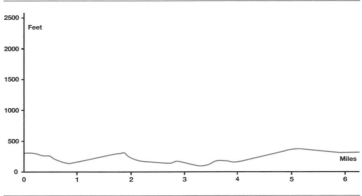

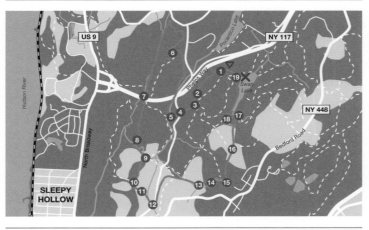

HIKE DESCRIPTION

Stroll along the impeccably maintained carriage roads of Rockefeller State Park Preserve and explore what was once a palatial estate. Then visit Captain Lawrence Brewing Company, the area's largest craft brewery, for a wide-ranging beer selection and excellent food.

The Rockefeller State Park Preserve was once owned by brothers William and John D. Rockefeller, co-founders of Standard Oil. In its early-20th-century heyday, the property encompassed over 1,000 acres and included Rockwood Hall, a 204-room mansion that was the second-largest private residence in the country. After the mansion was demolished in the 1940s, much of the property was deeded or sold to the state for recreation and preservation.

This hike provides an overview of the various areas of the park and their natural features. While there are no blazes to mark the trails, there are well-positioned signs at almost every intersection and there are free trail maps available at the visitor center. Start by crossing the parking lot to find Nature's Way, an undulating grassy path made intermittently uneven by emerging roots. While the footing is not challenging, this is the most technical section of the hike; the remainder of the carriage roads are wide, flat, crushed-gravel paths. A short walk leads to one of the largest glacial erratics in the Hudson Valley, a massive boulder left behind 10,000 years ago by the retreating glaciers of the last ice age. Like all erratics, it differs in composition from all other rocks in the area, and was likely carried from above the Arctic Circle by the flowing ice.

After visiting the Glacial Erratic, you'll soon come to Old Sleepy Hollow Road, the first of many carriage roads on the hike. This trail leads you downhill and over the Pocantico River, which you will then parallel for a short while before reaching the 13 Bridges Trail. This trail is one of the park's highlights and crosses a series of small footbridges over the meandering Gory Brook. Side trails in this section lead to the Old Croton Aqueduct, a nearby park that preserves the 41-mile aqueduct that supplied water to 19th-century residents of New York City.

As you move away from the Pocantico River, you'll enter an area of the park dominated by farmland before eventually coming upon the banks of Swan Lake. This 22-acre lake is the heart of the Preserve and is home to turtles, snakes, herons, and other migrating waterfowl. From the lake, it's a short walk back to the visitor center; alternatively, you can extend the hike by heading east and take in the sweeping vistas of Buttermilk Hill.

TURN-BY-TURN DIRECTIONS

1. From the visitor center, cross the parking lot and head northwest on Nature's Way.
2. At 0.3 miles, take a short spur trail on the right to the Glacial Erratic; then return to the main trail.
3. At 0.5 miles, make a right turn onto the Old Sleepy Hollow Road Trail and head downhill.
4. At 0.7 miles, cross an auto road and continue on the Old Sleepy Hollow Road Trail.
5. At 0.8 miles, cross a wooden footbridge over the Pocantico River and turn right onto the Pocantico River Trail.
6. At 1.5 miles, make a right onto the 13 Bridges Trail.
7. At 2.8 miles, cross under Route 117 and continue straight at the intersection onto the Gory Brook Road Trail.
8. At 3.2 miles, reach an intersection and make a right to continue on the Gory Brook Road Trail over a small footbridge. After crossing the bridge, make a left onto the Spring Trail.
9. At 3.4 miles, make a right onto Shady Lane and climb uphill.
10. At 3.6 miles, continue straight on the Douglas Hill Loop.
11. At 3.8 miles, continue left on the Douglas Hill Loop as it passes under a large stone bridge.
12. At 3.9 miles, after passing under the bridge (Sleepy Hollow Road), turn left on Hudson Pines Road.
13. At 4.6 miles, the trail forks; continue left on Hudson Pines Road, then head straight through an unmarked intersection.
14. At 4.7 miles, bear left and then right to continue on Hudson Pines Road through several intersections.
15. At 4.9 miles, make a hard left onto Greenrock Road.
16. At 5.2 miles, continue straight through a large intersection on Greenrock Road.
17. At 5.5 miles, make a hard left onto Brothers' Path.
18. At 5.6 miles, make a hard right to stay on Brothers' Path and follow this trail along the western edge of Swan Lake.
19. At 6.0 miles, reach a large intersection at the far end of the lake. Follow signs straight ahead to the visitor center.

FIND THE TRAILHEAD

From the Tarrytown train station, take Cortlandt Street north for 0.5 miles. Make a right on Beekman Avenue, then an immediate left onto Pocantico Street. Follow this for 0.3 miles to US 9/North Broadway. Make a left on US 9 and continue for 1.5 miles; then take the exit for NY-117 East toward Pleasantville. Take NY-117 East for 1.4 miles to the park entrance on the right. The parking lot is at the end of Tower Hill Road, with the visitor center on the left.

CAPTAIN LAWRENCE BREWING COMPANY

Founded by Scott Vaccaro in 2006, Captain Lawrence was at the forefront of the New York craft beer movement. Today, it is the largest brewery in the Hudson Valley, brewing 28,000 barrels a year and distributing across the East Coast and internationally. The brewery first gained acclaim for its award-winning sours, though today it is equally renowned for East Coast IPAs, lagers, and seasonal stouts. Both the indoor and outdoor tasting areas are expansive, and the brewery hosts weekly trivia nights and regular live music. The site is also the home of Current Spirits, a distillery under the same ownership.

LAND MANAGER

New York State Office of Parks, Recreation, and Historic Preservation
125 Phelps Way
Pleasantville, NY 10570
(914) 631-1470
www.parks.ny.gov/parks/rockefeller/details.aspx
Map: www.avenzamaps.com/maps/91893/

BREWERY/RESTAURANT

Captain Lawrence Brewing Company
444 Saw Mill River Road
Elmsford, NY 10523
(914) 741-2337
www.captainlawrencebrewing.com
Distance from trailhead: 6.1 miles

HOOK MOUNTAIN

HIKE ALONG A STUNNING RIDGELINE FAR ABOVE THE HUDSON RIVER

NYACK

▷⋯ STARTING POINT	⋯✕ DESTINATION
NYACK BEACH STATE PARK	**HOOK MOUNTAIN**
🍺 BREWERY	🏁 HIKE TYPE
MARLOWE ARTISANAL ALES	**MODERATE** 🚶
🐾 DOG FRIENDLY	📅 SEASON
YES (LEASH REQUIRED)	**YEAR-ROUND**
$ FEES	🕐 DURATION
$10/CAR (FREE WITH EMPIRE PASS)	**3 HOURS**
⛰ MAP REFERENCE	↦ LENGTH
POSTED AT TRAILHEAD	**6.1 MILES** (LOOP)
🔍 HIGHLIGHTS	〰 ELEVATION GAIN
RIDGELINE, RIVER PATH	**796 FEET**

EAGER TO SHARE PALE ALE

5.4 % ALCOHOL CONTENT

 HAZY YELLOW

CITRUS, ORANGE

FRUIT, MILD HOPS

BITTERNESS	SWEETNESS

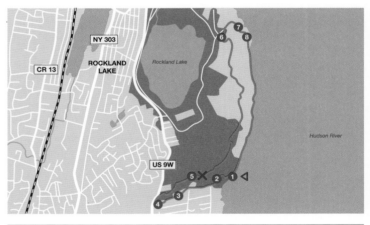

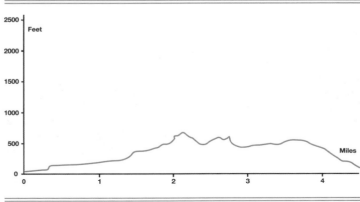

HIKE DESCRIPTION

This hike has a bit of everything: it begins with a steep climb, opens up to vistas as you traverse the rolling hills atop a cliff band, and finishes as a relaxing riverside stroll. Just down the road, Marlowe Artisanal Ales serves up high-quality, low-alcohol beers in a hip, contemporary, downtown setting.

Rising abruptly from the banks of the Hudson River, Hook Mountain is part of the Palisades Sill, a geologic formation of igneous rock that stretches from Staten Island north to Haverstraw. This more than 20-mile stretch of cliff bands towering over the western aspect of the river is easily visible from Manhattan and the George Washington Bridge. (The Palisades get their name because early Dutch settlers thought the cliffs looked like a fence. The native Lenape called this part of their ancestral home "Wee-Awk-En" or "rocks that look like trees," from where the town of Weehawken gets its name.)

Given their height, exposure, and strategic location along the river (and nearly atop the commercial center of New York), the Palisades played an important role in the Revolutionary War and were also the staging ground for numerous duels, including the infamous Burr-Hamilton duel (in Weehawken) of 1804. Extensive quarrying in the Palisades region yielded much of the stone used to build New York City before the area was protected by the Palisades Interstate Park Commission in 1911.

Hook Mountain lies near the northernmost aspect of the Palisades and is among its most striking features. This hike passes through a variety of terrain and puts the best of the mountain on full display. From the Nyack Beach parking lot, start north on the bike path along the river

and follow it briefly before making a sharp 180-degree turn onto the Hook Mountain Summit Path. The trail skirts the southern border of the park before climbing steeply to intersect with the Long Path. In under a mile, the Long Path reaches the summit of Hook Mountain, a flat, rocky plateau with a nearly panoramic view of the surrounding area: Rockland Lake to the north, Tarrytown to the east, and the Tappan Zee/ Mario Cuomo Bridge and New York City skyline to the south. The trail is rugged in spots but is well marked and easy to follow as it descends from the summit and traverses the Palisades ridgeline.

About two miles past the summit, the trail descends steeply over some tricky washed-out terrain before reaching a series of well-maintained stone steps leading to a paved road. On your left is the Rockland Lake Fire Company, established in 1862 as Knickerbocker Engine Company No. 1 and still active as one of the smallest and oldest firefighting units in the county. The Long Path continues northward, but you'll turn right on the paved road and head down a steep hill, curving gradually to the right. Follow the road south as it turns into a crushed gravel bike path and drops all the way down to the Hudson River. From here, it's less than two miles back to the car along a lovely riverside bike path with plenty of benches and picnic tables where you can stop and enjoy the views of the water.

TURN-BY-TURN DIRECTIONS

1. From the parking lot, head north on the bike path along the river for just under 0.1 miles before making a sharp left turn onto the ascending white-blazed Hook Mountain Summit Path.
2. At 0.3 miles, the trail reaches an auto road. Make a slight left and follow the road briefly downhill. Presently the white blazes continue across the road and to the right. Keep going on this flat/ undulating section for 0.75 miles.

3. At 1.0 miles, the trail swings right and heads steeply uphill on a series of well-hewn stone steps.
4. At 1.2 miles, the trail intersects the teal-blazed Long Path. Make a right and follow the Long Path northward.
5. At 1.8 miles, reach the summit of Hook Mountain. Continue north on the Long Path, past several unmarked spurs on the right, notably at 2.4, 3.4, and 3.6 miles.
6. At 4.0 miles, turn right onto the paved Rockland Lake Road and follow the road downhill.
7. At 4.3 miles, reach the bottom of the hill and continue straight/ south as the road transitions to a flat, gravel bike path.
8. At 4.4 miles, continue straight past a marked turn-off for Haverstraw Beach on the left. The path descends to the banks of the Hudson River and continues south to the Nyack Beach parking area.

FIND THE TRAILHEAD

From the NYS Thruway/I-87, take Exit 11 towards Nyack. Turn left on North Highland Avenue and follow it for 0.4 miles before making a right onto 6th Avenue. Continue for 0.5 miles until the road ends at North Broadway. Make a left on North Broadway and proceed for 1.8 miles to the park entrance. The trailhead is at the back of the parking area, at the bottom of the hill by the river.

MARLOWE ARTISANAL ALES

After amassing a decade of experience in the beer industry—at Pennsylvania's Voodoo Brewing Company and the Twelve Percent Beer Project in Connecticut—owner and head brewer Zac Ross opened Marlowe Artisanal Ales in 2022 as an homage to his grandfather. The brewery and tasting room are in the heart of downtown Nyack and are a popular destination for cyclists and day trippers from New York City. The exposed brick walls create a warm atmosphere for sampling Marlowe's flavorful, low-ABV brews and specialty tacos. The flagship Eager to Share pale ale is clean and crisp. Zac has created variations on his flagship theme by replacing the standard citra/mosaic hop mix with Nectaron hops, among other varieties, and regularly returns to other experimental beers, such as the annual anniversary porter, which is aged in 23-year-old Pappy Van Winkle barrels.

LAND MANAGER

Palisades Parks Conservancy
PO Box 24
New York, NY 10163-0024
(917) 246-2376
www.palisadesparks.org
Map: www.avenzamaps.com/maps/837756?utm_source=affiliate&utm_medium=affiliate_link&utm_campaign=apgar%40nynjtc.org&utm_term=1343509888

BREWERY/RESTAURANT

Marlowe Artisanal Ales
132 Main Street
Nyack, NY 10960
(845) 480-5495
www.marloweales.com
Distance from trailhead: 2.4 miles

JACKIE JONES MOUNTAIN LOOP

A SAMPLING OF ICONIC HIKING TRAILS

STONY POINT

▷··· STARTING POINT	···✗ DESTINATION
BIG HILL/JACKIE JONES TRAILHEAD	**BIG HILL**
🍺 BREWERY	🗺 HIKE TYPE
INDUSTRIAL ARTS BREWING COMPANY	**MODERATE** 🥾
🐾 DOG FRIENDLY	📅 SEASON
YES (LEASH REQUIRED)	**YEAR-ROUND**
$ FEES	🕐 DURATION
NONE	**2 HOURS 30 MIN.**
⛰ MAP REFERENCE	↦ LENGTH
HARRIMAN STATE PARK TRAIL MAP	**4.1 MILES** (LOOP)
🔍 HIGHLIGHTS	〰 ELEVATION GAIN
FIRE TOWER, RUINS, RUSTIC LEAN-TO	**709 FEET**

7.1 %
ALCOHOL
CONTENT

WRENCH IPA

HAZY

CITRUS

FRUITY,
DRY,
HOPPY

BITTERNESS

5
4
3
2
1

SWEETNESS

5
4
3
2
1

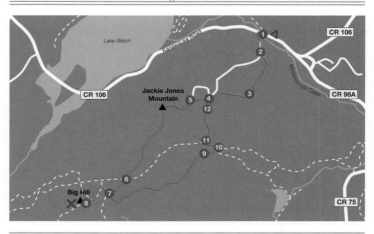

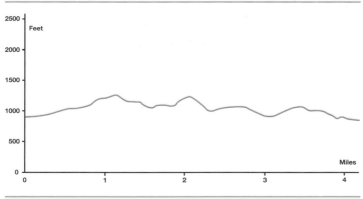

HIKE DESCRIPTION

For an entrée into the myriad hiking options in Harriman State Park, you can't do better than this tour of historic points of interest on iconic thru-hiking trails. For an entrée into the local beer scene, you can't beat Industrial Arts Brewing, a no-frills powerhouse interested only in brewing some of the state's best beer.

Harriman State Park—the second-largest in New York—is an outdoor refuge for residents of New York City and its suburbs. Harriman contains over thirty lakes (there are large public beaches at Lake Tiorati and Lake Welch) and over 200 miles of well-maintained hiking trails. Both the Appalachian Trail and the Long Path pass through Harriman, making it a haven for both day hikers and thru-hikers.

The first half of this loop follows the Suffern-Bear Mountain Trail, an historic route first opened in 1927 that spans the length of Harriman from north to south. After about half a mile following a paved, unmaintained access road and a brief singletrack section, you'll encounter the remains of the Orak Mansion. These stone ruins date to 1923, when the mansion was built by George Buchanan, a vice president of the Corn Products Refining Company. ("Orak" is "Karo" spelled backwards—the mansion was named after a corn sweetener.) The trail then climbs gradually but steadily for about a mile to the summit of Jackie Jones Mountain. The summit is marked by a 60-foot-tall fire tower, built in 1928, that is listed on the National Historic Lookout Register. The top of the tower affords unobstructed views of the New York City skyline on a clear day.

The trail descends gradually and then steeply through a well-shaded forest of pine and oak, crossing two small streams before levelling out and eventually reaching an intersection with the teal-blazed Long Path. The Long Path is another iconic New York footpath, stretching 351 miles from Manhattan to Albany. Following the Long Path downhill to the left will be your return route, but for the full hike, make a right turn and follow the joint blazes of the LP and the SBMT uphill towards Big Hill. You'll reach the Big Hill lean-to after a short, steep uphill climb. A bit further on, you'll come to a large rock outcropping with excellent views of Winterburne Hill and Horse Chock Mountain to the southeast and New York City to the south. Big Hill Shelter is a perfect spot for lunch before returning to the trailhead via the Long Path and the SBMT.

TURN-BY-TURN DIRECTIONS

1. From the parking area, head northwest along Kanawauke Road toward the Harriman State Park sign, crossing a small stream. Immediately after crossing the stream, make a left turn onto the yellow-blazed Suffern-Bear Mountain Trail (SBMT).
2. At the fork at 0.2 miles, continue left on the SBMT.
3. At 0.5 miles, reach an intersection with several small, unmarked trails. Continue following the SBMT to the right.
4. At 0.8 miles, come to a T-junction and follow the SBMT to the right. Presently, the trail curves left and climbs at a moderate grade.
5. At 0.9 miles, the trail skirts to the left of a radio tower and small building before reaching the summit fire tower at 1.1 miles. After exploring the tower, continue to follow the yellow blazes downhill to stream crossings at 1.3 and 1.5 miles.
6. At 1.6 miles, reach an intersection in a large clearing; continue straight, still following the yellow blazes.
7. At 1.8 miles, the SBMT intersects the teal-blazed Long Path (LP). To visit Big Hill Shelter, make a right turn at this intersection and follow the joint yellow and teal blazes uphill to the shelter.
8. At 2.0 miles, reach the Big Hill Shelter. To return, retrace your steps downhill to the intersection of the SBMT and the LP. Then leave the yellow-blazed trail and continue downhill and to the right, following the teal blazes.
9. At 3.0 miles, cross a stream on the left and head uphill.
10. At 3.1 miles, turn left and head uphill on the Old Turnpike Trail, where you will begin to see some light blue blazes.
11. At 3.2 miles, reach another intersection; make a right and continue slightly uphill to the east. There are no blazes to mark this section, but the path is wide and easy to follow.
12. At 3.4 miles, after a steady uphill climb, the path rejoins the yellow-blazed SBMT. (You may recognize this intersection from step 4 above.) Make a right turn and follow the yellow blazes back to the parking area.

FIND THE TRAILHEAD

From Exit 14 on the Palisades Interstate Parkway, head west on Willow Grove Road for 1.5 miles. Merge onto Kanawauke Road and continue 0.3 miles to the trailhead parking area on the left side of the road, just before the entrance to Harriman State Park.

INDUSTRIAL ARTS BREWING COMPANY

Industrial Arts has a factory-chic aesthetic befitting its surroundings and an unapologetic, all-about-the-beer ethos. The combination tasting room and brewing operation is housed in a huge converted warehouse with impossibly high ceilings and large windows that create a bright, open, and airy feel. Industrial Arts was founded in 2016 by Jeff O'Neill, who developed the iconic Flower Power IPA while working as the head brewer at Ithaca Beer. No surprise, then, that the signature

Wrench is one of the best examples of a hazy East Coast IPA there is. An explorative spirit drives the brewing process, and more than half of the twenty or so beers on tap at any one time are experimental offerings; on a recent visit we sampled not only IPAs but an ESB, a farmhouse sour, and a barleywine ale. There's no kitchen, but visitors are welcome to bring their own food from any of several restaurants housed in the nearby buildings.

LAND MANAGER

Harriman State Park
Seven Lakes Drive/Bear Mountain Circle
Ramapo, NY 10974
(845) 947-2444
www.parks.ny.gov/145
Map: www.parks.ny.gov/documents/parks/HarrimanTrailMap.pdf

BREWERY/RESTAURANT

Industrial Arts Brewing Company
55 W. Railroad Ave #25
Garnerville, NY 10923
(845) 942-8776
www.industrialartsbrewing.com
Distance from trailhead: 4.5 miles

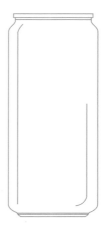

STERLING FURNACE

A SECLUDED FOREST HIKE WITH STONE RUINS AND HILLTOP VIEWS

TUXEDO

▷··· STARTING POINT	···✕ DESTINATION
FURNACE LOOP TRAILHEAD	**INDIAN HILL**
🍺 BREWERY	🏁 HIKE TYPE
FOREIGN OBJECTS BEER COMPANY	**MODERATE** 🥾
🐾 DOG FRIENDLY	📅 SEASON
YES (LEASH REQUIRED)	**YEAR-ROUND**
$ FEES	🕐 DURATION
NONE	**2 HOURS**
⛰ MAP REFERENCE	↦ LENGTH
POSTED AT TRAILHEAD	**3.9 MILES** (LOOP)
🔍 HIGHLIGHTS	〰 ELEVATION GAIN
STONE STRUCTURES, POND	**526 FEET**

HANGING GARDENS
DDH INDIA PALE ALE
MOSAIC, EL DORADO

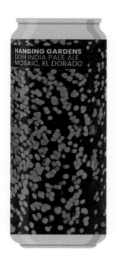

7.0 %
ALCOHOL
CONTENT

HANGING GARDEN PALE ALE

 HAZY YELLOW

CITRUS, HOPS

ORANGE, HOPPY

BITTERNESS

SWEETNESS

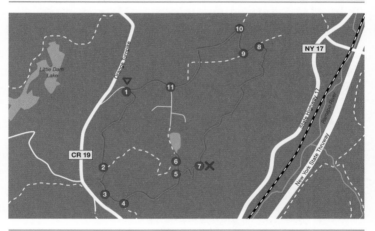

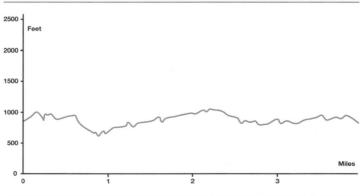

Feet

Miles

HIKE DESCRIPTION

A deceptively challenging loop that rewards hikers with views of nearby Harriman State Park. Just up the road, Foreign Objects Beer Company offers a creative, alchemical interpretation of classic American ales and farmhouse brews.

Just north of the New Jersey border, Sterling Forest State Park feels relatively isolated, despite being situated in the midst of several large population centers. Boasting similar topography to nearby Harriman State Park, Sterling Forest is significantly less developed and less frequently visited. The vast majority of park land is pristine forest habitat, a crucial refuge for timber rattlesnakes, black bears, foxes, and various migratory birds. Several lakes and reservoirs

also serve as important sources of water for the surrounding areas. Sterling Forest's hiking trails provide a sense of solitude not easily found in other nearby parks. Because this hike is relatively isolated, be sure to tell someone where you're going before you head out.

While the overall elevation gain is not extreme and there are no gigantic climbs, this hike features near-constant ups and downs, particularly over the course of its first half. You'll start climbing immediately after departing from the trailhead on the Indian Hill Loop Trail. For the first half-mile, the trail ascends at a fairly constant grade until it crests the hill in a small clearing with views of Tiger Mountain—home of the now-defunct Tuxedo Ridge Ski Center—and Bare Mountain, just to the south. From there, you'll pick up the Furnace Loop Trail, which descends steeply over rocky terrain to the ruins of the Southfield Furnace and Ironworks. This furnace was a smelting site for the iron ore mined nearby in the 19th century and was added to the National Register of Historic Places in 1973. The ruins are fenced off, but you can still appreciate the remains of the large structure that housed the furnace, as well as those of an old railroad crossing over the adjacent creek.

From here, the trail flattens briefly before climbing again to a junction with the Indian Hill Loop. A short detour to the left on the Warbler Trail leads to a small pond and the remains of an old dam, a picturesque spot for a picnic. Once refreshed, you'll return to the trail junction and continue on the Indian Hill Loop Trail, which presently climbs a series of stone plateaus to the top of Indian Hill. The summit is a wide rock ledge, providing excellent views of Harriman to the east. After leaving the summit, you'll have the majority of the climbing behind you, though the trail continues to undulate over the next two miles. You'll cross over and between a number of stone walls, remnants of the area's mining and agricultural past, before completing the loop on a wide, rocky roadbed that leads downhill to the trailhead.

TURN-BY-TURN DIRECTIONS

1. From the trailhead kiosk, head right on the yellow-blazed Indian Hill Loop and immediately begin climbing uphill.
2. At 0.6 miles, just past a clearing at the top of the hill, make a right on to the red-blazed Furnace Loop.
3. At 0.9 miles, reach the fenced-off ruins of Southfield Furnace on the right.
4. At 1.0 miles, the trail forks; bear left, continuing to follow the red-blazed Furnace Loop.
5. At 1.4 miles, rejoin the Indian Hill Loop. Turn left, following joint red and yellow blazes.
6. At 1.5 miles, the red-and-yellow blazed trail makes a hard left. Continue straight on the green-blazed Warbler Trail to a large pond. After visiting the pond, backtrack to the junction where the red and yellow blazes came together at 1.6 miles. Continue straight past the red-blazed trail on the right, now following the yellow-blazed Indian Hill Loop.
7. At 1.8 miles, reach the rock cairn marking the summit of Indian Hill.
8. At 2.7 miles, follow the Indian Hill Loop as the trail makes a hard left turn onto a wide doubletrack trail between two stone walls.
9. At 2.8 miles, continue to follow the yellow blazes as the trail makes a hard right and reverts to singletrack.
10. At 3.0 miles, reach a junction with the terminus of a blue-blazed trail on the right. Turn left, continuing to follow the yellow blazes.
11. At 3.6 miles, turn right onto an old roadbed and continue to follow the yellow-blazed Indian Hill Loop to return to the trailhead.

FIND THE TRAILHEAD

From I-87, take Exit 15A toward NY-17 North. Take NY-17 North for 8.8 miles. Turn left onto Orange Turnpike and follow it for 1.3 miles. At the sign on the right for Indian Hill, turn right onto a dirt road and follow it uphill for 0.2 miles until it ends in a small dirt parking area. The trailhead is located next to the kiosk at the front of the parking lot.

FOREIGN OBJECTS BEER COMPANY

Founded in 2017, Foreign Objects began in the wholesale business, brewing and distributing from various locations in the tri-state area before settling in the current brewhouse and taproom dubbed "The Nerve Center" in 2019. The brewery's branding philosophy is to pay homage to actual philosophy: its cans sport abstract art and its beer descriptions read like a Descartes treatise. The bar is decorated with a striking kintsugi-style tile backsplash, with exposed steel beams and ductwork offset by soft wood accents. The twenty taps rotate between a variety of styles, with many showcasing the brewery's signature "new-American hoppy ales," and also offer selections from other local breweries and cideries.

LAND MANAGER

NYS Department of Parks, Recreation, and Historic Preservation
116 Old Forge Road
Tuxedo, NY 10987
(845) 351-5907
www.parks.ny.gov/parks/sterlingforest/details.aspxMap:
Map: www.parks.ny.gov/documents/parks/SterlingForestTrailMap.pdf

BREWERY/RESTAURANT

Foreign Objects Beer Company
150 West Mombasha Road
Monroe, NY 10950
(914) 441-4484
www.foreignobjectsbeer.com
Distance from trailhead: 3.7 miles

SCHUNEMUNK MOUNTAIN

A CHALLENGING HIKE ALONG A RIDGE

CORNWALL

▷⋯ STARTING POINT	⋯✗ DESTINATION
OTTERKILL ROAD TRAILHEAD	**SCHUNEMUNK MOUNTAIN**
🍺 BREWERY	🔀 HIKE TYPE
RUSHING DUCK BREWERY	**STRENUOUS**
🐾 DOG FRIENDLY	📅 SEASON
YES (LEASH REQUIRED)	**YEAR-ROUND**
$ FEES	🕐 DURATION
NONE	**4 HOURS 15 MIN.**
⛰ MAP REFERENCE	↦ LENGTH
POSTED AT TRAILHEAD	**7.4 MILES** (LOOP)
🔍 HIGHLIGHTS	〰 ELEVATION GAIN
PANORAMIC VIEWS, ROCK FORMATIONS	**1,541 FEET**

 9.6 %
ALCOHOL CONTENT

IMPERIAL BEANHEAD PORTER

 BLACK

COFFEE

COFFEE

BITTERNESS

5
4
3
2
1

SWEETNESS

5
4
3
2
1

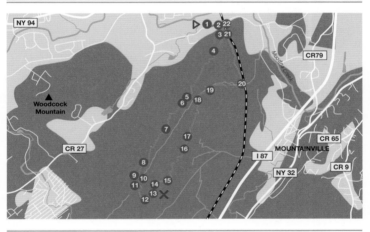

NY 94

▷ 1 2 22
3 21

4

CR79

Mccobb Creek

20

Woodcock Mountain

5 18 19

6

7

17

16

CR 27

8

9 10
11 14 15
12 13 ✕

CR 65

MOUNTAINVILLE

I 87

NY 32

CR 9

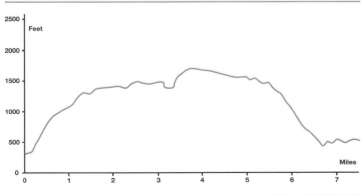

2500
Feet

2000

1500

1000

500

0

0   1   2   3   4   5   6   7

Miles

HIKE DESCRIPTION

Explore the ridgelines of 1,664-foot Schunemunk Mountain, the highest point in Orange County. Then visit Rushing Duck Brewery, where an extensive rotating tap list awaits.

From the trailhead, begin by hiking along Otterkill Road in the direction of the Moodna Viaduct, a nearly 200-foot-high railroad trestle. Before reaching the trestle, the trail makes an abrupt right, crossing the road and almost immediately becoming the aptly named Trestle Trail. This steep, rocky climb is interrupted about halfway up by a very short spur trail on the right, leading to a wooden bench with a spectacular view of the Shawangunks and Catskills to the north. Returning to the Trestle Trail, you'll continue climbing for another half-mile before gaining the ridgeline.

After about three miles, a short descent leads into Barton Swamp. Cross the bog on a series of log trestles and ascend to the eastern ridge of the mountain. This is a relatively short climb—less than half a mile in total—but is fairly steep in spots, with some small rocky scrambles. At the top, you'll walk the length of the ridge to the summit. Along the way, you'll be able to fully appreciate the unique rock that comprises this mountain. Alternately known as "puddingstone" (for its supposed resemblance to Christmas pudding) and Schunemunk conglomerate, it is made up of pebbles and small stones embedded in a greyish-red sandstone. This composite rock is distinct from that found elsewhere in the Hudson Valley.

Shortly past the summit, keep an eye out for a series of large rock cairns on the left, marking a spur trail to the Megoliths. These massive boulders likely cracked off the summit during the glacial melt. After nearly two undulating miles, the Jessup Trail descends steeply alongside Baby Brook. A small footbridge at the base of the descent crosses the brook and leads to the final mile of the loop.

TURN-BY-TURN DIRECTIONS

1. From the trailhead kiosk, head east on the white-blazed Trestle Trail, keeping Otterkill Road on the right.

2. At 0.2 miles, turn right to cross Otterkill Road and continue on the Trestle Trail.

3. At 0.3 miles, reach an intersection with the red-blazed Otterkill Trail. Turn and follow the Trestle Trail uphill.

4. At 0.7 miles, take a right on a short spur trail to Sharon's Bench; then return to the main trail and continue uphill.

5. At 1.6 miles, the Trestle Trail ends. Continue straight on the Barton Swamp Trail, marked by a white blaze with a red dot in the center.

6. At 1.7 miles, the trail forks. Bear left on the orange-blazed Western Ridge Trail.

7. At 2.2 miles, at a junction with the Sweet Clover Trail on the left, continue straight on the Western Ridge Trail.

8. At 2.7 miles, continue straight across a wide, unblazed private trail, remaining on the Western Ridge Trail.

9. At 3.0 miles, turn left onto the Ridge-to-Ridge Trail, blazed with a blue dot on a white background.

10. At 3.1 miles, cross over an unmarked doubletrack trail, continuing straight on the Ridge-to-Ridge Trail.

11. At 3.2 miles, turn left on the Ridge-to-Ridge Trail, crossing a marshy area before ascending toward the ridge.

12. At 3.5 miles, turn left onto the yellow-blazed Jessup Trail.

13. At 3.6 miles, reach the peak of Schunemunk Mountain. Continue on the Jessup Trail.

14. At 3.7 miles, turn left at a large rock cairn and follow a series of cairns to the Megoliths, before returning to the main trail and continuing northeast on the Jessup Trail.

15. At 4.0 miles, pass a junction on the right with the black-blazed Dark Hollow Trail and continue on the Jessup Trail.

16. At 4.7 miles, the white-blazed Sweet Clover Trail joins from the right. Follow the joint white and yellow blazes.

17. At 4.9 miles, the Sweet Clover Trail branches left. Continue straight on the Jessup Trail.

18. At 5.5 miles, reach Baby Brook. Turn right and follow the Jessup Trail downhill.

19. At 5.7 miles, the trail forks. Make a hard left to continue on the Jessup Trail.

20. At 6.3 miles, the Jessup Trail ends at an intersection with the Otterkill Trail at the bottom of the descent. Turn left on the red-blazed Otterkill Trail and cross a footbridge over Baby Brook.

21. At 7.1 miles, the Otterkill Trail ends at the junction with the white-blazed Trestle Trail from step 3. Continue straight on the Trestle Trail.

22. At 7.2 miles, cross Otterkill Road and turn left on the grassy trail to return to the trailhead.

FIND THE TRAILHEAD

From I-87 (NYS Thruway), take Exit 16 for NY-17/US-6 toward Harriman. Follow NY-17 West for 5.0 miles and take Exit 130 for NY-208. Bear right at the fork to take NY-208 North for 2.8 miles. Make a slight right onto Clove Road and follow it for 4.4 miles. Turn right onto Otterkill Road and proceed for 0.8 miles to the trailhead parking area on the left.

RUSHING DUCK BREWERY

Over the past decade, Rushing Duck has become a staple of the Hudson Valley craft beer scene while still maintaining its charm as a small, family-run brewery. The taproom, housed in a spacious converted warehouse, boasts twenty taps, allowing for ample experimentation beyond the long-running mainstays. Bean Head porter is a tasty quaff even if you don't like java, and is strong enough to be mistaken for a cup of joe if paired with steak and eggs. A large outdoor seating area hosts live music and other events in nice weather, and there are indoor acoustic performances and trivia nights throughout the year. Food trucks are on-site almost year-round, and outside food is allowed. Dogs are not permitted anywhere on the property.

LAND MANAGER

NYS Department of Parks, Recreation, and Historic Conservation
116 Old Forge Road
Tuxedo, NY 10987
(845) 351-5907
www.parks.ny.gov/parks/184/
Map: www.parks.ny.gov/documents/parks/SchunnemunckTrailMap.pdf

BREWERY/RESTAURANT

Rushing Duck Brewery
2 Greycourt Avenue
Chester, NY 10918
(845) 610-5440
www.rushingduck.com
Distance from trailhead: 11.5 miles

FULLER MOUNTAIN

AN ENJOYABLE HIKE IN A LIGHTLY TRAVELED PARK

WARWICK

▷··· STARTING POINT	···✕ DESTINATION
BOWEN ROAD TRAILHEAD	**FULLER MOUNTAIN**
🍺 BREWERY	🗺 HIKE TYPE
THE DROWNED LANDS	**MODERATE** 🥾
🐾 DOG FRIENDLY	📅 SEASON
YES (LEASH REQUIRED)	**YEAR-ROUND**
$ FEES	🕐 DURATION
NONE	**1 HOUR 30 MIN.**
⛰ MAP REFERENCE	↦ LENGTH
POSTED AT TRAILHEAD	**2.6 MILES** (ROUND-TRIP)
🔍 HIGHLIGHTS	〜 ELEVATION GAIN
WETLANDS, STREAM CROSSINGS, VIEWS	**253 FEET**

4.8 %
ALCOHOL
CONTENT

GATHER HOUSE
WITBIER

 HAZY YELLOW

 CITRUS,
WHEAT,
MARSHMALLOW

 ORANGE,
GRASSY,
MILD SPICE

BITTERNESS

SWEETNESS

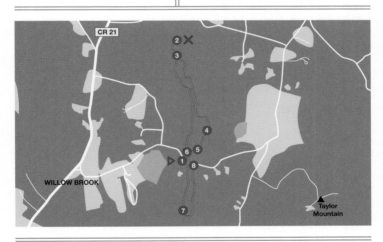

CR 21

WILLOW BROOK

Taylor
Mountain

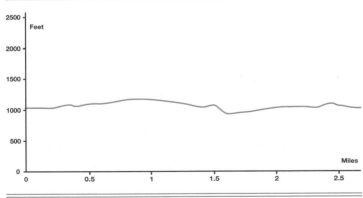

2500

Feet

2000

1500

1000

500

0

Miles

0   0.5   1   1.5   2   2.5

HIKE DESCRIPTION

Discover the hidden gem that is Fuller Mountain, a short but surprisingly demanding hike through a small forest preserve. Then discover another hidden gem: the Drowned Lands, the state's best brewery you've never heard of.

Just north of the New Jersey state line, Fuller Mountain Preserve is a small sylvan oasis in an area traditionally dominated by farmland and agriculture. The primary features within the forest are Fuller Mountain (alternately known as Round Hill), a 1,200-foot prominence near the park's northern end, and Fuller's Brook (also called Deckertown Brook or Curtie Cantine Brook), which runs the length of the preserve before draining into Wawayanda Creek. Both are named for James Fuller, one

of the property's early owners. Previously, the hilltop had been a look-out point for the native Lenape tribe—and later Revolutionary War soldiers—to monitor the valley below. The park is home to small reptiles and amphibians and several mammals, including long-tailed weasels and the occasional black bear.

There are two loops of trails, one on either side of the centrally located trailhead, making this hike a figure-of-eight with the parking area located at the midpoint. Begin by crossing the road from the parking area and following the orange markers north, climbing gradually but fairly steadily toward the top of Round Hill. The winding trail is some-what rocky and muddy in spots, but the footing is generally secure. You'll reach the summit in less than a mile, where you'll find a wooden observation platform as well as the stone ruins of a 19th-century cabin built by Colonel Victor Wilder, who owned the property before Fuller. From the platform, the view of the Walkill Valley is buttressed by War-wick Mountain to the east and the long, double-ridged expanse of Schunemunk Mountain to the northeast.

The return trip down the Creek Trail is more circuitous and technically challenging than the initial climb, as numerous undulations and rocky stretches make this section both tricky and enjoyable. You'll drop down into the ravine twice to traverse the creek by hopping over a series of rocks. The trail is generally dry, despite its proximity to the brook, but you'll notice an abundance of moss on the rocks and trees in this area. It's about a mile from the summit back to the car, at which point you can begin the second part of the hike, following the orange blazes through the southern aspect of the preserve. The first quarter mile of trail in this section is wider, with relatively smooth footing, until it reaches the brook on the left. After crossing the stream, you'll face a short but steep climb up the eastern slope of the ravine. From here, the trail involves a bit of side-hill footing and numerous rocky segments on the mostly downhill return to the trailhead.

TURN-BY-TURN DIRECTIONS

1. From the parking area, cross Bowen Road and head north on the orange-blazed Fuller Mountain Trail. Immediately pass an intersection with a green-blazed trail on the right and continue straight.
2. At 0.8 miles, reach the summit of Fuller Mountain. There is a viewing platform just beyond the summit. From there, retrace your steps back downhill.
3. At 1.0 miles, turn left on the green-blazed Creek Trail.
4. At 1.5 miles, cross the stream over a series of rocks.
5. At 1.8 miles, cross the stream again and continue on the Creek Trail.
6. At 1.9 miles, rejoin the Fuller Mountain Trail and turn left to cross the road and return to the parking area. Continue the hike by leaving the opposite side of the parking area and heading south on the Fuller Mountain Trail's South Loop.
7. At 2.2 miles, cross the stream and follow the trail uphill.
8. At 2.6 miles, the trail exits the woods onto Bowen Road about 100 feet east of the parking area. Turn left and cross the stream on the road to return to the car.

FIND THE TRAILHEAD

From NY-17, take Exit 124 for NY-17A/County Road 106. Follow NY-17A West for 12.5 miles. Turn left onto Ball Road and follow it for 0.8 miles. Turn left onto Brady Road and follow it for 2.1 miles. Turn right onto Bowen Road and proceed for 0.5 miles to the parking area on the left side of the road. Do not park on Bowen Road—you will be towed!

THE DROWNED LANDS

Since it opened in late 2020, The Drowned Lands has built a reputation as one of the state's finest craft breweries. The name refers to the agricultural traditions of the Warwick Valley, where decades of frequent flooding have produced the rich "black dirt" for which the area is renowned. Owner Mike Kraai is committed to the winemaking concept of terroir, which involves incorporating flavors and characteristics from the natural environment into the brewing process. Much of the beer is fermented in oak barrels or foeders, which lends it a distinctive taste. Kraai's passion for quality has not gone unnoticed. At the 2022 TAP NY beer festival, The Drowned Lands was awarded the FX Matt Cup as the best brewery in New York, and its Gather House won the Gold Medal for wheat beers. The brightly lit tasting room, housed in a century-old brick building that was once a reform school, has been updated with modern flourishes and hanging plants and strikes a perfect balance between rustically chic and casually elegant. An expansive back patio opens onto the banks of Wawayanda Creek, a bucolic setting for an afternoon tasting.

LAND MANAGER

Orange County Land Trust
50 Ogden Drive
Mountainville, NY 10953
(845) 534-3690
www.oclt.org
Map: www.oclt.org/orange-county-land-trust-new-york/wp-content/uploads/2021/02/Fuller-Mountain-Map-OCLT-FINAL.pdf

BREWERY/RESTAURANT

The Drowned Lands
251 State School Road
Warwick, NY 10990
(845) 986-2337
www.drownedlands.beer
Distance from trailhead: 7.4 miles

MIDDLETOWN RESERVOIR LOOP

TRAVERSE VARIED TERRAIN AROUND A SERIES OF LAKES

MIDDLETOWN

▷⋯ STARTING POINT	⋯✗ DESTINATION
MIDDLETOWN RESERVOIR RED TRAIL START	**HIGHLAND LAKE**
🍺 BREWERY	🁢 HIKE TYPE
EQUILIBRIUM BREWERY	**MODERATE**
🐾 DOG FRIENDLY	📅 SEASON
YES (LEASH REQUIRED)	**YEAR-ROUND**
$ FEES	🕐 DURATION
NONE	**2 HOURS 45 MIN.**
⛰ MAP REFERENCE	↦ LENGTH
POSTED AT TRAILHEAD	**6.9 MILES** (LOLLIPOP)
🔎 HIGHLIGHTS	〜 ELEVATION GAIN
LAKES	**568 FEET**

4.8 %
ALCOHOL
CONTENT

PHOTON PALE ALE

HAZY GOLD

HOPS,
MILD FRUIT

PINEAPPLE,
MILD HOPS

BITTERNESS	SWEETNESS

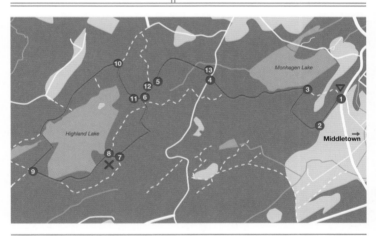

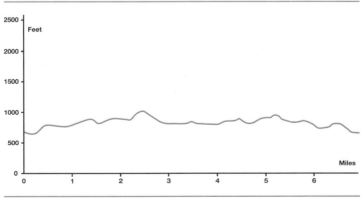

HIKE DESCRIPTION

Explore these brand-new trails surrounding a series of lakes that supply the drinking water to the nearby city—water that helps the brewers at nearby Equilibrium Brewery craft some of the most delicious beers in the state.

The trail system at the Middletown Reservoir is a new addition to the local hiking scene. The city opened up the 1,250-acre watershed for public use in 2020. The eight miles of hiking trails are the first step in a larger plan for the development of a public park, which includes an expansion of the trail network.

Rather than starting from the main parking area, you'll begin at an alternate trailhead that provides access to the full length of the Red Trail (all the trails in the system are named for the colors of their blazes), in the more rugged and less-accessed section of the park. The trail begins as a wide doubletrack path that is mostly flat with the exception of a short, steep climb about half a mile in. After about three quarters of a mile, the trail transitions to a rocky singletrack and snakes along the shore of Monhagen Lake. There is a rock outcropping at the

western end of the lake with a nice view. From there, the trail angles uphill and becomes more technical before reaching a road crossing and the main parking area.

Continuing from the back of this parking area, you'll pick up the White Trail, which undulates gently for about half a mile before intersecting with the Blue Trail. Make a left on the Blue Trail to begin your loop around Highland and Shawangunk Lakes. This section boasts smoother footing than earlier portions of the hike but is still technical in spots. A longer climb leads through a beautiful section of white pines along a short ridgeline. You'll then drop back downhill and proceed clockwise around Highland Lake as the trail transitions to dirt road for most of the circumnavigation of the reservoir. Notice the extensive remains of 19th-century stone walls along the left side of the road, evidence that this area has been providing drinking water to local residents for over 150 years. A flat bit of singletrack trail completes the loop and returns you to the White Trail and then to the main parking area, from where you can retrace your steps on the Red Trail back to the start.

TURN-BY-TURN DIRECTIONS

1. Leave the parking area to the left of the interpretive sign and follow signs for the Red Trail.
2. At 0.2 miles, continue to follow the Red Trail as it angles uphill and to the right.
3. At 0.7 miles, turn left to follow the Red Trail as it transitions to rocky single track and descends toward the lake.
4. At 1.5 miles, continue past a metal gate, cross the road, and enter the main parking area for this trail system. Exit through the back of the parking lot following the White Trail.
5. At 2.0 miles, continue straight ahead on the Blue Trail.
6. At 2.1 miles, turn left to stay on the Blue Trail.
7. At 2.7 miles, reach an intersection with the Orange Trail on your left. Make a right to continue on the Blue Trail towards the lake.
8. At 2.8 miles, the Blue Trail ends at an intersection with the Black Trail. Turn left on the Black Trail, following the lake clockwise.
9. At 3.4 miles, make a right on a dirt road.
10. At 4.5 miles, turn right onto the Black Trail.
11. At 4.8 miles, turn left onto the Blue Trail.
12. At 4.9 miles, continue straight onto the White Trail.
13. At 5.4 miles, reach the main parking area. Cross back over the road and retrace your steps on the Red Trail to arrive back at the start.

FIND THE TRAILHEAD

From I-84, take Exit 15B for US-6 West/NY 17M West toward Middletown. Follow Route 17M West for 0.4 miles. Turn left on Route 108 and follow it for 0.3 miles to a traffic circle. Take the second exit off the circle onto County Road 78. Drive 2.3 miles to the trailhead parking area on the left.

EQUILIBRIUM BREWERY

The founders of Equilibrium Brewery are constantly striving for balance: between "massive flavor" and drinkability, and between scientific principles and community experience. Peter Oates and Ricardo Petroni, both MIT-trained environmental engineers, spent nearly eight years perfecting their recipes before opening the brewery in 2017. The current site opened in 2019 and boasts a beautiful taproom, expansive outdoor seating, and a fantastic BBQ menu. The beer names are an homage to the owners' scientific backgrounds, and a huge mural of Albert Einstein adorns the side of the building. Many of the beers have won national and international recognition, including Photon, a flavorful yet eminently quaffable pale ale.

LAND MANAGER

City of Middletown Department of Recreation and Parks
16 James Street
Middletown, NY 10940
(845) 346-4100
www.middletown-ny.com/en/departments/recreation-parks/parks.html
Map: www.middletown-ny.com/en/departments/recreation-parks/recreation-documents/3238-reservoir-map-quick-download/file.html

BREWERY/RESTAURANT

Equilibrium Brewery
4 South Street
Middletown, NY 10940
(845) 956-0211
www.eqbrew.com
Distance from trailhead: 2.2 miles

THREE LAKES LOOP

A HIDDEN GEM INSIDE A POPULAR STATE PARK

PUTNAM VALLEY

▷⋯ STARTING POINT	⋯✕ DESTINATION
DENNYTOWN ROAD, FAHNESTOCK STATE PARK	**HIDDEN LAKE**
🍺 BREWERY	🔲 HIKE TYPE
SLOOP BREWING COMPANY	**EASY**
🐾 DOG FRIENDLY	📅 SEASON
YES	**YEAR-ROUND**
💲 FEES	🕐 DURATION
NONE	**1 HOUR 45 MIN.**
⛰ MAP REFERENCE	↦ LENGTH
CLARENCE FAHNESTOCK MEMORIAL STATE PARK TRAIL MAP	**3.6 MILES** (LOOP)
🔎 HIGHLIGHTS	〰 ELEVATION GAIN
LAKES, WILDLIFE	**160 FEET**

JUICE BOMB IPA

6.5 % ALCOHOL CONTENT

HAZY

FRUITY

CITRUS, HOP BITE

BITTERNESS

SWEETNESS

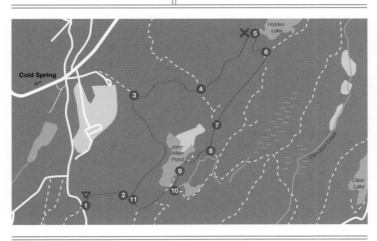

Hidden Lake

Cold Spring

John Allen Pond

Canopus Creek

Clear Lake

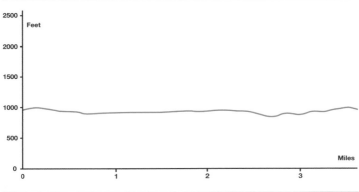

HIKE DESCRIPTION

 Ramble through the forest down an old railroad bed to visit a collection of small lakes and ponds frequented by birds, beavers, and other wildlife. Then stop in for a hazy Juice Bomb at Sloop Brewing, one of the area's largest and most successful craft breweries.

Clarence Fahnestock Memorial State Park is a haven for outdoor enthusiasts that offers hiking, fishing, birding, boating, camping, and even a network of maintained Nordic ski trails in the winter. Most of the activities are clustered around the park offices and campground on the eastern edge of the park near the Taconic State Parkway. This slightly more remote hike hews to the central area of the park, which, while still popular, sees far less foot traffic.

Starting from the back of the small parking area off Dennytown Road, you'll follow a short, unmarked trail to Sunken Mine Road, a well-maintained dirt road that will deposit you at the start of the Old Mine Railroad Trail. This track trail follows the route of a narrow-gauge railroad that served nearby iron mines in the mid 19th century. Keep an eye out for old mine dumps along the way.

The Old Mine Railroad Trail follows the western shore of John Allen Pond, affording some pleasant views of the lake and a large beaver dam (particularly if you follow a short, unmarked spur on your right about three-quarters of a mile in). After leaving the shoreline, the trail becomes slightly more technical, with some roots emerging from the otherwise smooth rail bed. Continue meandering past reedy marshes, replete with birds and croaking bullfrogs, until you reach the southern end of Hidden Lake. This clearing, just past the halfway point of this hike, is a beautiful spot for a picnic or a rest while you scout the area for birds, beavers, and turtles.

Past Hidden Lake, the trail becomes narrower and wilder, though it is still well-maintained and easy to follow. A short distance after the lake, the Old Mine Railroad Trail terminates at an intersection where you'll turn right onto the Three Lakes Trail. As you follow this twisting trail through some old-growth forest back towards John Allen Pond, you'll get nice views from its opposite shore. After nearly a mile, the trail crosses a stream. Be careful on the rocks in the spring, as the snowmelt can make this crossing a bit dicey. A little way past the stream, the trail ends back at Sunken Mine Road. Turn right, keeping the pond on your right, and follow the road to the initial intersection with the Old Mine Railroad Trail. Stay on Sunken Mine Road until you reach the parking area.

TURN-BY-TURN DIRECTIONS

1. From the back corner of the parking area, follow a small, unmarked singletrack trail a very short distance to Sunken Mine Road, a wide dirt road. Turn right and follow the road uphill and then downhill.

2. At 0.3 miles, turn left on the yellow-blazed Old Mine Railroad Trail.

3. At 1.0 miles, turn right, continuing to follow the yellow blazes on a wider, flat rail bed.

4. At 1.3 miles, the trail intersects with the red-blazed Charcoal Burners Trail; continue straight on the yellow-blazed Old Mine Railroad Trail.

5. At 1.8 miles, reach a small clearing with a beautiful view of Hidden Lake directly ahead; the trail makes a hard right, keeping the lake to its left.

6. At 2.0 miles, the yellow-blazed Old Mine Railroad Trail ends at an intersection with the blue-blazed Three Lakes Trail. Make a right and follow the blue blazes.

7. At 2.4 miles, pass an intersection with the red-blazed Charcoal Burners Trail on your right, continuing straight on the blue-blazed Three Lakes Trail.

8. At 2.7 miles, the trail makes a hard left. A very short spur on the right leads to an excellent view of John Allen Pond.

9. At 2.9 miles, bend to the right and carefully cross a stream before climbing briefly uphill. A small unnamed pond can be glimpsed through the trees on the left.

10. At 3.0 miles, rejoin Sunken Mine Road and make a right. Pass a guardrail on the right with a small sandy beach abutting the lake just beyond.

11. At 3.3 miles, reach the start of the Old Mine Railroad Trail on your right; continue straight and uphill on Sunken Mine Road to return to the parking area.

FIND THE TRAILHEAD

From the Cold Spring Depot train station, head east on Main Street/Route 301 for 5.4 miles. Turn right on Dennytown Road and follow it southward for 0.7 miles. The parking area is just off the road on your left.

SLOOP BREWING COMPANY

Working out of a small garage in nearby Poughkeepsie in 2012, founders Adam Watson and Justin Taylor could hardly have imagined that, in less than a decade, Sloop Brewing would grow into one of the region's largest and most successful craft breweries. The current location opened in 2018 inside one of the many remnants of the IBM infrastructure scattered around the Mid-Hudson Valley. While there is no outdoor seating area, there is ample space inside the massive facility for long communal tables, cornhole, video games, pinball, and live music. True to their motto "Open to Adventure," the brewmasters consistently incorporate new ingredients into the beermaking process, and there are always experimental beers among the dozen-plus taps in the tasting room. While the signature Juice Bomb is a fruity IPA not to be missed, you'd be well-advised to check out the award-winning sour Confliction Ale too. The kitchen is not averse to a bit of adventure, either, and serves up wood-fired pizzas, burgers, fusion bowls, and more.

LAND MANAGER

Clarence Fahnestock Memorial State Park
1498 Route 301
Carmel, NY 10512
(845) 225-7207
www.parks.ny.gov/parks/133/details.aspx
www.parks.ny.gov/documents/parks/ClarenceFahnestockTrailMap.pdf

BREWERY/RESTAURANT

Sloop Brewing Co.
755 East Drive #106
East Fishkill, NY 12533
(518) 751-9134
www.sloopbrewing.com
Distance from trailhead: 11.3 miles

MOUNT BEACON

A CHALLENGING CLIMB ON AN INCLINE RAILWAY BED LEADS TO A HISTORIC FIRE TOWER

BEACON

▷··· STARTING POINT	···✗ DESTINATION
MOUNT BEACON TRAILHEAD PARKING AREA	**MOUNT BEACON FIRE TOWER**
🍺 BREWERY	HIKE TYPE
HUDSON VALLEY BREWERY	**STRENUOUS**
🐾 DOG FRIENDLY	📅 SEASON
YES (LEASH REQUIRED)	**YEAR-ROUND**
$ FEES	🕐 DURATION
NONE	**2 HOURS 30 MIN.**
⛰ MAP REFERENCE	↦ LENGTH
POSTED AT TRAILHEAD	**3.9 MILES** (ROUND-TRIP)
🔍 HIGHLIGHTS	〰 ELEVATION GAIN
FIRE TOWER, HISTORIC RUINS	**1,377 FEET**

INCANDENZA
SOUR IPA

6.0 % ALCOHOL CONTENT

 HAZY GOLD

GRASSY, LEMON ZEST

CITRUS

BITTERNESS   SWEETNESS

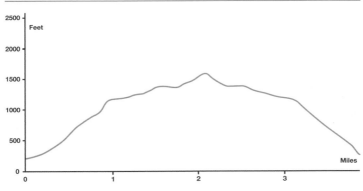

BEACON

NY 9D

North Beacon Mountain

Beacon Reservoir

South Beacon Mountain

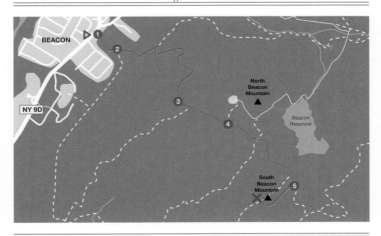

Feet

Miles

HIKE DESCRIPTION

Take a steep, strenuous climb up Mount Beacon for some of the best views in the state. Afterward, visit the town of Beacon, which offers an eclectic mix of shops, restaurants, galleries, and, of course, innovative sour beers at Hudson Valley Brewery.

The climb to the fire tower atop South Mount Beacon is among the more popular hikes in this book. With a world-renowned modern art museum, numerous parks and open spaces, and a downtown full of bespoke shops and farm-to-table cuisine, the town of Beacon is a favorite weekend destination for those looking to escape the bustle of the city. The Metro North rail line provides easy access to Beacon's many wonderful offerings, including the Hudson Highlands, a diverse, non-contiguous state park on the river's eastern shore. The highest point in the Highlands, the fire tower, is an obvious destination for hikers eager to take in some of the most expansive views in the Hudson Valley.

The hike to the tower is not only steep but steeped in history. The trail roughly parallels the course of the Mount Beacon Incline Railway, which was the steepest railway in the world when it opened in 1902. This funicular railway carried tourists to the top of the mountain for several decades. The heyday of the Incline Railway occurred in the 1920s, when over 100,000 people per year visited the Beaconcrest Hotel and Casino, which were built on the mountainside in 1926. The fire tower was built in 1931 and was used for fire detection until the early 1970s. It was added to the National Lookout Historic Register in 2005 and restored in 2013.

Begin your hike by leaving the back of the parking lot, passing by a wooden gate and following the gravel Casino Trail. Within just a few minutes, you'll come upon some of the ruins of the rail bed; soon afterward, you'll reach a set of two hundred or so metal stairs. Here's where the hard

work begins! The first mile of the climb includes several rocky switch-backs. Ignore multiple marked and unmarked side trails and follow the Casino Trail until you reach—you guessed it—the Casino! Or, rather, what's left of it. The remains of a large brick structure on the right near the one-mile mark were once the top of the funicular, and you can enter the old structure to see the massive pieces of equipment still inside. The old casino site is just below these ruins. You can reach it by following a short staircase down to the left, which leads to a beautiful overlook.

Past these ruins, the trail widens and levels out significantly; while there is still some climbing to come, the worst is most definitely behind you. In less than half a mile, you'll reach a large intersection; continue to follow the red blazes as the trail narrows and becomes rockier and steeper once again. Presently, a large clearing will open up, revealing a view of the fire tower directly ahead. A few minutes later, you'll reach an inter-section with an unmarked trail to the right that makes a direct beeline for the tower. Resist the temptation to take this path and continue for just a minute on the red-blazed trail until you reach the white-blazed Summit Trail on the right. From here, it's a short but punchy climb to the tower.

The views from the top of the tower are truly spectacular. On a clear day, you can see 75 miles in any direction. Most proximally, the Hudson Highlands stretch before you to the south, and the wide expanse of the Newburgh-Beacon Bridge crossing the Hudson is visible to the west. Looking further, you'll see the distant peaks of the Catskills and, beyond them, the Adirondacks to the northwest, as well as glimpses of New York City on a clear day.

TURN-BY-TURN DIRECTIONS

1. Leave the parking lot by passing through a wooden gate and follow the red-blazed Casino Trail.
2. At 0.2 miles, climb a long series of metal stairs.
3. At 1.0 miles, reach the remains of the incline rail house; explore carefully before continuing on the Casino Trail.
4. At 1.3 miles, follow the red blazes straight/slightly right through a large intersection; the trail dips briefly downhill before resuming the climb at a moderate grade.
5. At 1.8 miles, take the white-blazed Summit Trail to the right and follow this to the summit fire tower at 2.0 miles. Retrace your steps to return to the parking area.

FIND THE TRAILHEAD

From the Beacon Metro North train station, follow Railroad Drive to Beekman Street, which turns into Wolcott Avenue after 0.5 miles. Follow Wolcott Avenue for 1.1 miles to the Scenic Hudson parking area directly ahead of you. The City of Beacon offers a free Loop Bus from the train station to the trailhead every 30 minutes

HUDSON VALLEY BREWERY

Jason Synan and Mike Renganeshi earned their stripes as brewers working at the Brewery at Bacchus while they were students at SUNY New Paltz. They opened the Hudson Valley Brewery with local John Anthony Gargiulo in 2016. The trio converted a 200-year-old abandoned factory in downtown Beacon into one of the most highly regarded breweries in the region. They specialize in farmhouses and sours; the Incandenza puts an intriguing sour spin on the East Coast IPA style. The brewers are constantly evolving both flavor combinations and techniques such as barrel aging, and most of their ingredients are sourced locally. There's no kitchen, but outside vendors provide wood-fired pizzas in the tasting room. Please note that while the brewery offers both indoor and outdoor seating, dogs are not allowed (with the exception of service animals).

LAND MANAGER

Scenic Hudson
One Civic Center Plaza, Suite 200
Poughkeepsie, NY 12601
845 473 4440
www.scenichudson.org
www.scenichudson.org/wp-content/uploads/2019/10/Mt.Beacon.webmap.png

BREWERY/RESTAURANT

Hudson Valley Brewery
7 E. Main Street
Beacon, NY 12508
(845) 218-9156
www.hudsonvalleybrewery.com
Distance from trailhead: 1 mile

WALKWAY LOOP

AN URBAN HIKE ACROSS A TOWERING PEDESTRIAN BRIDGE

POUGHKEEPSIE

▷⋯ STARTING POINT	⋯✕ DESTINATION
POUGHKEEPSIE TRAIN STATION	**ZEUS BREWING COMPANY**
🍺 BREWERY	🏛 HIKE TYPE
ZEUS BREWING COMPANY	**EASY** 🚶
🐾 DOG FRIENDLY	📅 SEASON
NO	**APRIL–NOVEMBER**
$ FEES	🕐 DURATION
NONE	**1 HOUR 30 MIN.**
⛰ MAP REFERENCE	↦ LENGTH
WALKWAY LOOP TRAIL MAP	**3.1 MILES** (POINT-TO-POINT)
🔍 HIGHLIGHTS	〰 ELEVATION GAIN
BRIDGES, GLASS ELEVATOR	**339 FEET**

7.0 %
ALCOHOL CONTENT

URBAN OASIS SOUR

 GOLD

 APPLE

 APPLE, LIME ZEST

BITTERNESS

5
4
3
2
1

SWEETNESS

5
4
3
2
1

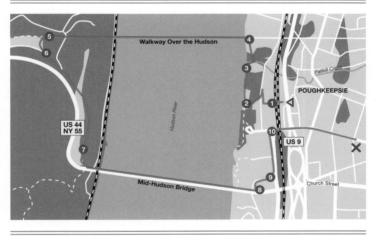

5
6
Walkway Over the Hudson
4
3
POUGHKEEPSIE
Fallkill Creek
2
1
US 44
NY 55
Hudson River
10
US 9
7
9
Mid-Hudson Bridge
8
Church Street

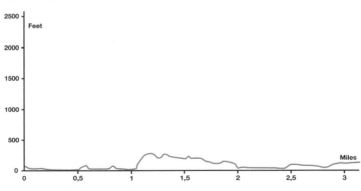

2500 Feet
2000
1500
1000
500
0

0   0,5   1   1,5   2   2,5   3

Miles

HIKE DESCRIPTION

Nearly $40 million was spent restoring the old Poughkeepsie–Highland Railroad Bridge and repurposing it for pedestrians, and walking across it is a breathtaking experience. Visit the rooftop deck at Zeus Brewing Company for another vantage point on the city, the river, and the bridges themselves.

When the Poughkeepsie–Highland Railroad Bridge first opened in 1889, its nearly 1.5-mile span made it the longest bridge in the world. Passing more than 200 feet above the water, the railroad ferried both passengers and cargo across the Hudson River for nearly a century until a fire destroyed much of the track and the underlying span in 1974. The restored bridge was opened as a state park in 2009; at the time of its reopening, it was the world's longest pedestrian bridge. Renamed the Walkway Over the Hudson, the park now attracts more than half a million visitors annually and is listed on the National Register of Historic Places.

The most intriguing means of accessing the Walkway is via the glass-enclosed elevator that brings visitors from the Poughkeepsie waterfront to the span above. This is also the easiest point of access from the Metro North train station. It affords a close-up view of the original steel girders that have supported the bridge for over a century. However, the elevator has limited operating hours, and is closed in the winter; furthermore, while leashed dogs are allowed on the Walkway, only service animals are permitted in the elevator. Plan accordingly and make sure to check the operating hours online before heading off. If your hike cannot include a

ride on the elevator, you can start from the parking lot on Parker Avenue in Poughkeepsie (just a ten-minute uphill walk from the train station), or on the western end of the span in Highland.

After riding the elevator, take your time crossing the Walkway from east to west. Admire the breathtaking views and read the interactive signs that provide historical context about the area. The western aspect of the bridge literally runs through the treetops of Franny Reese State Park and is especially striking when the leaves change color in autumn. There are bathrooms at either end of the bridge.

You'll leave the Walkway at this point and follow Haviland Road to the Mid-Hudson Bridge, where a pedestrian pathway provides your return route to Poughkeepsie. A short jaunt through town brings you to Main Street, where you'll see the train station directly ahead of you. It's barely a third of a mile up the road from here to the Zeus Brewing Company, which means an easy downhill stroll back to the train after you've quenched your thirst.

TURN-BY-TURN DIRECTIONS

1. Use the pedestrian walkway above the train tracks to leave the station through the parking garage. Exit to the west onto North Water Street. Cross the street and head downhill toward the waterfront on a paved access road.
2. At 0.2 miles, reach the waterfront; make a right on the sidewalk and head north.
3. At 0.3 miles, pass a skatepark on your right. Continue just a bit further on the sidewalk as it turns to the right. Immediately afterward, reach the Fall Kill Footbridge on the left. Cross the footbridge and follow the stone path directly ahead and to the left toward the elevator access path.
4. At 0.4 miles, reach the Walkway Elevator. Ride the elevator to the top. It's very cool! Upon exiting the elevator, turn left onto the walkway and head west over the river.
5. At 1.2 miles, come to the western end of the Walkway in Highland. There are bathrooms on your right. Make a left and head toward the parking area.
6. At 1.3 miles, just after the parking area, turn left and head downhill on Haviland Road, following signs for Franny Reese Park.
7. At 1.7 miles, the road ends at Johnson-Iorio Memorial Park. Follow the sidewalk straight ahead and left to join the pedestrian path over the FDR/Mid-Hudson Bridge.
8. At 2.4 miles, make a left turn off the pedestrian path onto a ramp with a fence on either side. Follow it downhill and to the left, where it terminates at Gerald Drive; make a right.
9. At 2.6 miles, make a left turn onto Rinaldi Boulevard.
10. At 2.8 miles, reach Main Street. The train station is directly ahead. Make a right turn on Main Street and head uphill, immediately crossing the bridge over the train tracks and then climbing steadily until you reach Zeus Brewing Company on your right at 3.1 miles.

FIND THE TRAILHEAD

There are multiple trains daily from Grand Central to Poughkeepsie. If traveling by car, park at the free Walkway parking area on Parker Avenue (parking at the train station isn't cheap) and start your hike from there.

ZEUS BREWING COMPANY

Zeus opened its doors in 2020. The youngest of several craft breweries in Poughkeepsie, it has already established itself as a real titan of the local beer scene. (Get it?) The first-floor dining area and bar have a clean, open feel. The main fermentation tanks are visible just off the dining room. When the weather is nice, you can ride the brewery's elevator to the rooftop deck, which is fully equipped with the same dozen beers that are on tap downstairs and provides fabulous views of the city, the river, and both bridges you just crossed. The beer selection is varied and includes IPAs, pilsners, lagers, and stouts. Urban Oasis is a lime and ginger sour with a surprisingly sweet and fruity taste. The kitchen serves up better-than-average pub fare, and the burgers and brick-oven pizzas are not to be missed.

LAND MANAGER

NYS Office of Parks, Recreation, and Historic Preservation
625 Broadway
Albany, NY 12207
(518) 474-0456
www.parks.ny.gov
Map: www.walkway.org/visit/walkway-loop-trail

BREWERY/RESTAURANT

Zeus Brewing Company
178 Main Street
Poughkeepsie, NY 12601
(845) 320-4560
www.zeusbrewingco.com
Distance from trailhead: 0.4 miles

FDR/VANDERBILT LOOP

A RIVERSIDE HIKE LINKING TWO ICONIC
19TH-CENTURY ESTATES

HYDE PARK

▷⋯ STARTING POINT

FRANKLIN D. ROOSEVELT HISTORIC SITE

⋯✕ DESTINATION

VANDERBILT MANSION

🍺 BREWERY

MILL HOUSE BREWING COMPANY

🧗 HIKE TYPE

MODERATE 🥾

🐾 DOG FRIENDLY

YES

📅 SEASON

YEAR-ROUND

$ FEES

NONE

🕐 DURATION

4 HOURS

⛰ MAP REFERENCE

POSTED AT TRAILHEAD

↦ LENGTH

9.0 MILES (LOLLIPOP)

🔍 HIGHLIGHTS

MANSIONS, HISTORIC SITES

〰 ELEVATION GAIN

482 FEET

4.6%
ALCOHOL
CONTENT

KOLD ONE KOLSCH

 CLEAR YELLOW

 YEAST

 WHEAT

BITTERNESS	SWEETNESS

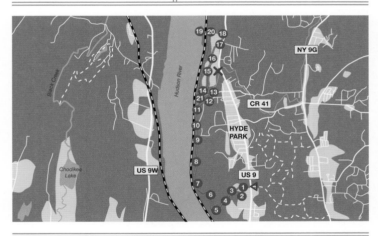

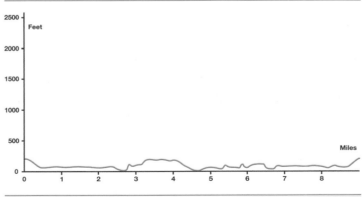

HIKE DESCRIPTION

Explore the home of the 32nd president of the US and stroll along the river to a neighboring estate of the Vanderbilt family. Visit Mill House Brewing Company for great beers and a varied menu that outstrips the regular pub menu fare.

This is a hike history buffs won't want to miss. You'll start from the visitor center at the Franklin D. Roosevelt National Historic Site. The grounds include the Roosevelts' 18th-century mansion, the presidential library and museum, well-maintained gardens, and miles of hiking trails.

The first section of this hike winds through the forest at the western aspect of the estate on carriage roads before emerging onto River Road. Along this stretch, you'll pass the Hyde Park Railroad Station. This stop on the New York-to-Albany line was first established in 1851, and the current structure dates to 1914. The last train stopped there in 1958, but the building has been restored and is now a railroad museum.

From the station, you'll head uphill to the south entrance of the Vanderbilt Historic Site, passing the Coach House (originally the stables and later storage for carriages and automobiles) and then the gardens before reaching the Vanderbilt Mansion itself. Built in 1896, the mansion is one of dozens constructed by the descendants of Cornelius Vanderbilt, a Gilded Age shipping and railroad magnate. In the early 20th century, the Vanderbilts were the wealthiest family in the world. Tours of the mansion run most days, and the grounds are open daily.

Continuing past the mansion, you'll head toward the northern edge of the estate before descending to the river. A short detour over the train tracks leads to Bard Rock. This outcropping is named for John Bard, a prominent 18th-century surgeon and the principal founder of Bard College in nearby Annandale. This parcel housed the Vanderbilt's boathouse and is a lovely spot for a picnic. After leaving Bard Rock, you'll join the Hyde Park Trail, which parallels the river heading southward, before rejoining River Road and retracing your steps back to the Roosevelt site.

TURN-BY-TURN DIRECTIONS

1. Leave the visitor center, passing the statue of Franklin and Eleanor Roosevel, and turn right on a small gravel footpath. Follow signs for the Springwood/Hyde Park Trail.

2. At 0.1 miles, turn right on the gravel path following signs for the Hyde Park Trail. The path passes the gardens before transitioning to pavement and continuing downhill.

3. At 0.2 miles, turn left at a gravel fork and head off the paved path, following the green-and-white markers of the Hyde Park Trail.

4. At 0.3 miles, turn right, following signs for the Hyde Park Trail and the Vanderbilt Estate.

5. At 0.5 miles, pass the yellow-blazed Meadow Trail on the left and continue on the Hyde Park Trail.

6. At 0.8 miles, the trail forks; stay left, following signs for the Hyde Park Trail and the Vanderbilt Estate.

7. At 1.4 miles, the trail makes a sharp right. Ignore the unmarked trail straight ahead and follow the Hyde Park Trail to the right.

8. At 1.8 miles, continue straight/north on River Road.

9. At 2.3 miles, the road forks; bear left and downhill, following the disks.

10. At 2.5 miles, make a left off the paved road onto a grassy path that leads through Riverfront Park.

11. At 2.6 miles, reach the Hyde Park Train Station at the north end of Riverfront Park. Rejoin River Road and continue north.

12. At 2.9 miles, turn left on Coach House Road to enter the Vanderbilt estate. Pass the Coach House on the right.

13. At 3.0 miles, cross a stone bridge and turn left.

14. At 3.1 miles, make a hard right turn onto a singletrack trail marked by the white-and-green disks of the Hyde Park Trail.

15. At 3.4 miles, reach the Vanderbilt Mansion. Pass behind the mansion, keeping it on the right.

16. At 3.7 miles, continue straight on Vanderbilt Park Road.

17. At 4.0 miles, continue straight on the road through a wooden gate. The road bears downhill and left toward the river.

18. At 4.3 miles, reach the bottom of the hill, with the gravel Hyde Park Trail on the left. Continue straight on the road over the bridge crossing the railroad tracks.

19. At 4.5 miles, reach the parking area for Bard Rock and explore the small peninsula before heading back across the bridge.

20. At 4.9 miles, turn right onto the gravel Hyde Park Trail.

21. At 6.0 miles, the trail ends on a private road. Turn left and head uphill.

22. At 6.1 miles, make a right over the stone bridge from step 13 above.

23. At 6.3 miles, exit the Vanderbilt estate and turn right, heading downhill on River Road. From here, retrace your steps past the train station and back to the start.

FIND THE TRAILHEAD

From the Mid-Hudson Bridge in Poughkeepsie, head north on US Route 9 North for 5.1 miles. Turn left onto FDR Drive, following signs for the Roosevelt estate, and follow it for 0.4 miles to the visitor center parking lot. The trail starts from the south patio of the visitor center, by the statue of Franklin and Eleanor Roosevelt on a park bench.

MILL HOUSE BREWING COMPANY

Since 2018, Poughkeepsie has experienced a craft beer explosion, with five new breweries opening in the last few years. Mill House predates them all by half a decade and serves up classic brews in a beautiful brick building that has housed various eateries over the past fifty years. Brewmaster Jamie Bishop developed the flagship kolsch years before the brewpub opened its doors. Today Mill House has expanded to a second brewing facility up the road in order to support distribution throughout the northeast. An on-site smoker and brick oven support an extensive restaurant menu.

LAND MANAGER

National Park Service
4097 Albany Post Road
Hyde Park, NY 12538
(845) 229-5320
www.nps.gov/hofr/index.htm
Map: www.hydeparkny.us/DocumentCenter/View/2659/Hyde-Park-Trail-System-Map-PDF?bidId=

BREWERY/RESTAURANT

Mill House Brewing Company
289 Mill Street
Poughkeepsie, NY 12601
(845) 485-2739
www.millhousebrewing.com
Distance from trailhead: 5.7 miles

RIVER TO RIDGE TRAIL

A PLEASANT RURAL STROLL ON A MULTI-USE TRAIL STEEPED IN HISTORY

NEW PALTZ

▷⋯ STARTING POINT	⋯✕ DESTINATION	
CARMINE LIBERTA BRIDGE	**TESTIMONIAL GATEHOUSE**	
🍺 BREWERY	🔠 HIKE TYPE	
YARD OWL CRAFT BREWERY	**EASY**	🚶
🐾 DOG FRIENDLY	📅 SEASON	
YES (LEASH REQUIRED)	**YEAR-ROUND**	
$ FEES	🕐 DURATION	
NONE	**3 HOURS 30 MIN.**	
⛰ MAP REFERENCE	↦ LENGTH	
POSTED AT TRAILHEAD	**7.6 MILES** (ROUND-TRIP)	
🔍 HIGHLIGHTS	〰 ELEVATION GAIN	
HISTORIC BUILDING, RIDGE VIEWS	**362 FEET**	

YARD OWL
BREWERY

5.0%
ALCOHOL
CONTENT

GRISETTE

 PALE STRAW

FRUITY

DRY,
MILD HOPS

BITTERNESS

SWEETNESS

5
4
3
2
1

5
4
3
2
1

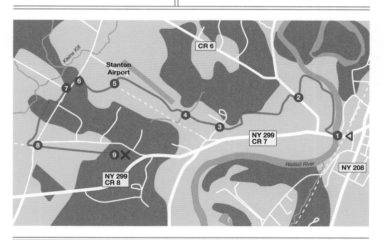

CR 6

Stanton
Airport

7 6

5

2

4

3

NY 299
CR 7

1

8

9

Wallkill River

NY 208

NY 299
CR 8

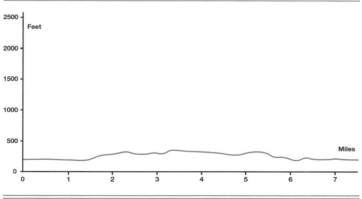

Feet

2500

2000

1500

1000

500

0

Miles

0   1   2   3   4   5   6   7

HIKE DESCRIPTION

Just steps from the oldest street in America, stroll through open fields on a wide crushed-gravel trail linking the historic town of New Paltz to the rock climber's paradise of the Shawangunk Ridge. Then, visit Yard Owl for hand-crafted, small-batch Belgian brews.

The town of New Paltz was founded by French Huguenot refugees in 1678 and is among the oldest continuously inhabited settlements in the US. Visitors can take in a number of historic sites, including Historic Huguenot Street (a collection of stone houses dating to the early 18th century), as well as evidence of the area's rich Native American tradition.

The River-to-Ridge Trail, established by the Open Space Institute in 2018, makes a perfect starting point for exploring the town and the rich diversity of outdoor opportunities that it provides. It begins on the western edge of the village, just steps from the Wallkill Valley Rail Trail and a short walk from both the historic district and the bus station, which provides daily service to and from New York City. The path is mostly flat and well-graded, and the striking landscape of the Shawangunk Ridge is visible throughout the majority of the hike.

The first mile follows the meandering path of the Wallkill River, then leaves the riverbank, crossing a road and skirting the northern edge of the Wallkill View Farm hay fields. In late summer, visit the fields just to the south for pictures in front of the towering sunflowers that grow along the cornfields.

A short climb opens onto a scenic, rolling, mile-long loop, featuring excellent views of Smiley Tower atop the ridge. It's not unusual to see red-tailed hawks hunting overhead, and foxes are often spotted darting through this field. The trail eventually terminates at Lenape Lane; make a left to reach the wide boulevard known as Pin Oak Allee, where a mostly flat stroll between the towering oak trees leads to the Testimonial Gatehouse. This distinctive stone structure was built in 1907 to welcome wealthy patrons to the Mohonk Mountain House, several miles uphill. Visitors were transported by horse-drawn carriage from the Gatehouse to the castle-like hotel atop the ridge at Mohonk Lake. The Gatehouse is an excellent spot for a mid-hike picnic. There is a parking lot with restrooms to the right. Retrace your steps to return back to the trailhead in downtown New Paltz.

The trail is open throughout the year; when conditions permit in the winter it is groomed by volunteers for Nordic skiing, and hikers are asked to use snowshoes so as not to damage the track.

TURN-BY-TURN DIRECTIONS

1. From the trailhead, head west across the Carmine Liberta Bridge, crossing the Wallkill River.
2. At 0.8 miles, pass the Springtown Road parking lot and cross Springtown Road.
3. At 1.6 miles, cross Lewis Lane, a small paved road, and climb uphill.
4. At 1.8 miles, the trail forks, eventually comprising a loop; bear right over a small footbridge.
5. At 2.4 miles, reach the apex of the loop. Head downhill to your right.
6. At 2.8 miles, follow the trail as it crosses Butterville Road and bear to the left over another footbridge.
7. At 2.9 miles, cross Pine Road and continue straight and slightly uphill.
8. At 3.2 miles, the trail reaches Lenape Lane, a wide dirt road. Head left over the newly restored pedestrian bridge to recross Butterville Road. (A right turn on Lenape will lead to a vast network of trails in the Mohonk Preserve, about 1 mile up the road. Be prepared to pay a day use fee for pedestrians and cyclists if you enter the Preserve.)
9. Continue for 0.6 miles to reach the Testimonial Gatehouse at 3.8 miles, before returning the way you came.

FIND THE TRAILHEAD

From the New Paltz bus station in the center of town, the trailhead at the Carmine Liberta Bridge is a 0.3 mile walk west/downhill on Main Street. By car, take Exit 18 off the NYS Thruway/I-87 North. Make a left at the light onto Main Street and drive 1.6 miles to the trailhead at the edge of town. Make a right onto Huguenot Street and drive 0.3 miles to a free municipal lot on the left.

YARD OWL CRAFT BREWERY

The Wallkill Valley is chock-full of small breweries. Our favorite local beer is in nearby Gardiner, where a small slice of Belgium is nestled in an industrial park just behind the Wallkill Valley Rail Trail. An easy walk or bike ride down the rail trail leads right to the back door of Yard Owl, a family-owned nanobrewery offering small-batch, handcrafted Belgian-style beers. As a licensed "Farm Brewery," Yard Owl brews most of its beers using ingredients from New York State and ages some varieties in spent wine barrels from a nearby vineyard. The Grisette is a light-bodied Belgian style with wonderful floral notes. The back door of the brewery opens onto the rail trail and a large lawn with picnic tables for outdoor seating and lawn games. In-house food offerings include beer-battered pretzels, pickled vegetables, and charcuterie. Owner and head brewer James Walsh mans the grill on busy summer weekends, making burgers or pulled pork sandwiches.

LAND MANAGER

Open Space Institute
1350 Broadway, Suite 201
New York New York 10018
(212) 290-8200
www.openspaceinstitute.org
Map: www.openspaceinstitute.org/places/river-to-ridge-trail

BREWERY/RESTAURANT

Yard Owl Craft Brewery
19 Osprey Lane
Gardiner, NY 12525
(845) 633-8576
www.yardowlcraftbrewery.com
Distance from trailhead: 5.0 miles

HIGH PETERS KILL TRAIL

VISIT ONE OF THE STATE'S TALLEST WATERFALLS IN AN ECOLOGICALLY DIVERSE PARK

GARDINER

▷⋯ STARTING POINT	⋯✗ DESTINATION
PETERS KILL TRAILHEAD	**AWOSTING FALLS**
🍺 BREWERY	🏞 HIKE TYPE
ROUGH CUT BREWING CO.	**MODERATE**
🐾 DOG FRIENDLY	📅 SEASON
YES (LEASH REQUIRED)	**YEAR-ROUND**
$ FEES	🕐 DURATION
$10/CAR (FREE WITH EMPIRE PASS)	**3 HOURS 30 MIN.**
🗺 MAP REFERENCE	↦ LENGTH
POSTED AT TRAILHEAD	**4.4 MILES** (LOOP)
🔍 HIGHLIGHTS	〜 ELEVATION GAIN
WATERFALL, SWIMMING HOLE	**488 FEET**

5.6%
ALCOHOL
CONTENT

MINNEWASKA
TRAIL PALE ALE

 COPPER

CITRUS

DRY,
CLEAN,
MILD HOPS

BITTERNESS

SWEETNESS

5
4
3
2
1

5
4
3
2
1

US 44
NY 55

Peterskill Falls

Awosting Falls

LAKE
MINNEWASAKA

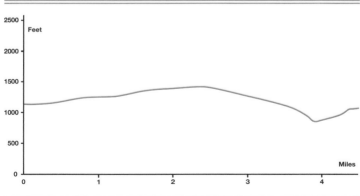

HIKE DESCRIPTION

The grandeur of Awosting Falls is only the appetizer on this varied hike, which cuts through swaths of wild blueberries and rare dwarf pine forests. Save room for food at Rough Cut Brewing Company, where in-the-know locals flock for post-hike beer and eats.

The Shawangunk Ridge (pronounced Shon-gum, and often referred to as "the Gunks") is a 50-mile-long geologic formation that stretches from northern New Jersey into the mid-Hudson Valley. The most recognizable feature of the Gunks is the Trapps, a 250-foot-tall vertical face of hard conglomerate rock that stretches for several miles along the western edge of the Walkill Valley. Carved by receding glaciers and fissured with deep crags, the Trapps are famous among rock climbers worldwide (and are a protected habitat for endangered peregrine falcons). The Gunks boast an incredible range of geological and natural diversity, including exposed ridges, glacial lakes, and rare dwarf-pine forests. Black bears are often spotted feasting on wild blueberries in the spring, and barred owls, red-tailed hawks, and bald eagles are common sightings throughout the year.

Awosting Falls is one of the most-visited sites along the ridge, and is relatively easy to reach from the Peters Kill trailhead. You'll leave the parking lot and (carefully!) cross the busy Route 44/55 to reach a short, rooty singletrack trail that leads to the wide, crushed-gravel carriage roads that make the Gunks a premier destination for runners, hikers, and cyclists. Most of these trails were built by hand in the mid-to-late 1800s to make possible recreational rides on horse-drawn carriages. Following the carriageway gradually uphill for about a mile, you'll reach Awosting Falls, which at 65 feet high is one of the tallest uninterrupted waterfalls in the state. It's an impressive sight any time of year, but is particularly striking in the spring, when the water volume is highest due to snowmelt. The flat rocks near the base make a perfect spot for a picnic. (Be sure to obey the park's carry-in/carry-out rules, and note that swimming near the falls is not allowed.)

To complete the loop, you'll continue uphill along the carriage road. A steeper climb leads to the top of the falls, where you can turn around and peer over the edge of the drop itself. After crossing several parking areas, you'll join the High Peters Kill trail and head north. The trail traverses beautiful open rock slabs pocked with dwarf pitch pines and hemlock.

The trail is well-marked and easy to follow, though it can be rugged in spots. It generally slopes gently downhill, affording expansive views of the Peters Kill Valley to the right. In late spring and early summer, wild blueberries bloom along the side of the trail. Be careful picking them, though; it's not unusual to encounter rattlesnakes along this section of the trail. While the rattlers will generally leave you alone, it's best not to step on one!

After about a mile and a half, the trail descends much more sharply down to the Peter's Kill, crossing the stream on a series of wooden footbridges. You may venture down to the stream to wade or refill your water bottles; on hot days you'll usually find bathers in the pools near the bridges. Be careful of slippery rocks if you decide to join them. Leaving the deep valley of the stream, you'll ascend steeply back to the park entrance, where you'll likely see climbers attempting tricky bouldering problems just off the trail.

TURN-BY-TURN DIRECTIONS

1. Leave the Peters Kill parking area via the auto entrance and immediately cross over Route 44/55 to the white-blazed Awosting Falls Connector Footpath.

2. At 0.2 miles, the connector path ends; make a right turn onto the wide carriage way of Trapps Road and begin a gradual uphill climb.

3. At 1.3 miles, reach the base of Awosting Falls. Those seeking a less strenuous hike can turn back here and return to the parking area.

4. At 1.5 miles, after a steeper uphill climb, reach the main park entrance. Continue straight across the park auto road and follow a paved, unmarked footpath.

5. At 1.8 miles, reach the Lower Awosting Parking Lot. Follow signs near the lot entrance to the High Peters Kill Trail. A short walk will take you back across Route 44/55 to the start of the blue-blazed High Peters Kill Trail.

6. At 3.7 miles, reach the footbridges crossing the Peters Kill. Make a right turn after the second bridge, continuing to follow the blue blazes.

7. At 3.8 miles, stay right at the fork on the yellow-blazed trail toward "Peters Kill Parking Lot."

8. At 4.0 miles, the yellow-blazed path ends; make a gentle left onto the red-blazed Red Loop Footpath toward the parking lot. It is a short but fairly steep climb from here to the finish.

FIND THE TRAILHEAD

Drive west out of New Paltz (exit 18 off the NYS Thruway) for 6.0 miles to the end of Route 299. Make a right turn on Route 44/55 and continue for 3.3 miles. The trailhead/parking area will be on your right.

ROUGH CUT BREWING COMPANY

This small, rustic hideaway, perched halfway up the western aspect of the Shawangunk Ridge, is a favorite among locals for its varied beer selection and a food menu that rivals those of much larger brew pubs. The beer choices are inventive and eclectic; you'll find a strong Belgian influence, but also smooth IPAs, malty stouts, and porters. A recently expanded tasting room opens onto a sizeable area in the rear for full dining; there is also plentiful outdoor seating including some well-shaded picnic tables.

LAND MANAGER

Minnewaska State Park
5281 Route 44/55
Kerhonkson, NY 12446
(845) 255-0752
www.parks.ny.gov/parks/minnewaska/details.aspx
Map: www.parks.ny.gov/documents/parks/MinnewaskaMinnewaskaState
ParkTrailMap.pdf

BREWERY/RESTAURANT

Rough Cut Brewing Company
5945 Route 44/55
Kerhonkson, NY 12446
(845) 626-9838
www.roughcutbrewing.com
Distance from trailhead: 5.3 miles

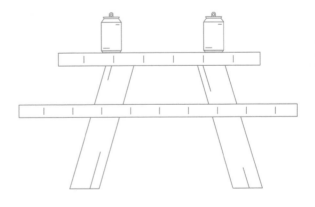

WILLOWEMOC WILD FOREST

TWO PONDS IN A WILD FOREST

LIVINGSTON MANOR

▷⋯ STARTING POINT	⋯✗ DESTINATION
FRICK POND TRAILHEAD ON BEECH MOUNTAIN ROAD	**HODGE POND**
🍺 BREWERY	HIKE TYPE
CATSKILL BREWERY	**MODERATE** 🚶
🐾 DOG FRIENDLY	📅 SEASON
YES (LEASH REQUIRED)	**YEAR-ROUND**
$ FEES	🕐 DURATION
NONE	**3 HOURS**
⛰ MAP REFERENCE	↦ LENGTH
POSTED AT TRAILHEAD	**6.8 MILES** (LOOP)
🔍 HIGHLIGHTS	〰 ELEVATION GAIN
PONDS, STREAMS, PINE FOREST	**825 FEET**

5.5 %
ALCOHOL CONTENT

NIGHTSHINE
BLACK LAGER

👁	BLACK
👃	MALT, NUTS
👄	COFFEE, CHOCOLATE

BITTERNESS

5
4
3
2
1

SWEETNESS

5
4
3
2
1

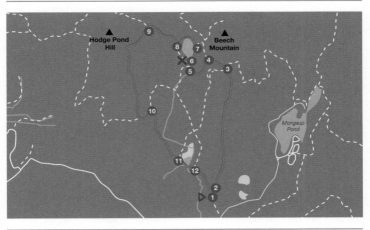

Hodge Pond Hill

Beech Mountain

9
8 7
6 4
5 3
10
Mongaup Pond
11
12
2
1

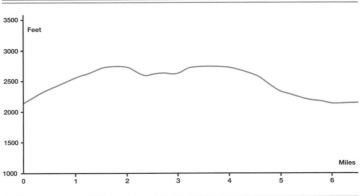

3500
3000
2500
2000
1500
1000

Feet

Miles

0   1   2   3   4   5   6

HIKE DESCRIPTION

Explore hilly terrain within a remote forest preserve tucked in the southwest corner of the Catskill Park. Then visit Catskill Brewery to sample its array of German and Belgian-influenced beers in a sustainable, community setting.

A bit off the beaten path for most visitors to the Catskills, Willowemoc Forest is a haven for outdoor recreation. Hunting and fishing are among the most popular activities. The preserve boasts five ponds and lakes open to anglers, as well as Willowemoc Creek, which locals claim as the "birthplace of fly-fishing in the US." (The creek runs through the nearby town of Roscoe, a world-renowned fishing destination known as "Trout Town USA.") Willowemoc's thirty miles of snowmobile trails comprise the largest such system in the Catskills. Over forty miles of trails are open for hiking, including trail connections to the Big Indian Wilderness, home of several Catskill High Peaks, which borders Willowemoc to the north.

This hike provides a taste of the designated "Forever Wild" forest in the preserve and visits two ponds that are popular hiking destinations. While hilly, the trail is not as steep or rugged as those you'll find elsewhere in the Catskills, and the paths and intersections are very well marked. Begin by following the Flynn Trail, a wide doubletrack that follows the bed of an old forest road. The trail climbs gradually but steadily uphill until it enters the Beech Mountain Nature Preserve. This private landholding contains both Beech Mountain, which, at 3,117 feet, is the highest summit in Sullivan County, and Hodge Pond. A state easement provides hikers access to this section of the trail. The secluded pond is a beautiful destination and a nice spot for a swim.

Past Hodge Pond, the route flattens as you turn onto the Quick Lakes Trail and is mostly downhill on the return trip to the trailhead. You'll hike through thick stands of pine and mixed deciduous forest. Keep an eye out for foxes and black bears. This section of the trail can get quite wet and muddy, particularly after the spring snowmelt; waterproof hiking boots are recommended. About a mile from the finish, you'll reach Frick Pond, another idyllic spot for a dip before you make your way back to the car.

TURN-BY-TURN DIRECTIONS

1. From the parking area, head north on the blue-blazed Flynn Trail.
2. At 0.1 miles, bear right to continue on the Flynn Trail.
3. At 1.7 miles, cross the yellow-blazed Big Rock Trail and continue straight on the Flynn Trail.
4. At 1.9 miles, the trail forks; bear left to stay on the Flynn Trail.
5. At 2.3 miles, the trail forks; bear right to stay on the Flynn Trail.
6. At 2.4 miles, reach Hodge Pond. Follow the trail to the right, heading counterclockwise around the pond.
7. At 2.6 miles, the trail forks. Bear left to stay on the Flynn Trail, keeping the pond on the left.
8. At 3.0 miles, make a hard right, leaving the shoreline of the pond and continuing on the blue-blazed Flynn Trail.
9. At 3.5 miles, the Flynn Trail ends at Junkyard Junction, an intersection with the red-blazed Quick Lake Trail. Turn left and follow the Quick Lake Trail southwest.
10. At 5.1 miles, reach Iron Wheel Junction, an intersection with the Logger's Loop on the left. Turn right to stay on the Quick Lake Trail toward Frick Pond.
11. At 5.9 miles, pass an intersection with the yellow-blazed Big Rock Trail and continue straight. Presently, arrive at Frick Pond on the left.
12. At 6.1 miles, reach Gravestone Junction. Pass the Logger's Loop on the left and continue straight to return to the trailhead.

FIND THE TRAILHEAD

From NY-17, take Exit 96 toward Livingston Manor. At the end of the ramp, turn left onto Debruce Road and follow it for 5.5 miles. Make a slight right as Debruce Road becomes Willowemoc Road; then make an immediate left onto Mongaup Road. Follow it for 2.7 miles and make a slight left onto Beech Mountain Road. In 0.3 miles, the road ends with the trailhead parking area on the left.

CATSKILL BREWERY

Less than a mile from downtown Livingston Manor, Catskill Brewery has built a loyal following of beer enthusiasts by combining "honest, hardworking beer" with sustainable brewing practices. The main brewhouse, a giant steel barn, is Gold LEED-certified, and the owners pay particular attention to water conservation and renewable energy sources. Most of the beer is brewed with local ingredients, and many brews are named for nearby Catskill peaks and landmarks. Nightshine, a German Schwarzbier, won a bronze medal at the World Beer Cup in 2022. Burgers, tacos, and other favorites are available at the on-site Catskill Food Truck. (Special menus are available when the truck travels to events in the local community.) The brewery also features two on-site accommodations, the "Brewmasters Cottage" and the "Microbrew Cabin," that can be reserved via Airbnb. If you're looking for even more beer, you can also check out Upward Brewing, barely a mile away on the south side of town.

LAND MANAGER

NYS Department of Environmental Conservation
21 South Putt Corners Road
New Paltz, NY 12561
(845) 256-3076
www.dec.ny.gov/lands/9146.html
Map: www.dec.ny.gov/docs/lands_forests_pdf/recmapwwwf.pdf

BREWERY/RESTAURANT

Catskill Brewery
672 Old Route 17
Livingston Manor, NY 12758
(845) 439-1232
www.catskillbrewery.com
Distance from trailhead: 9.1 miles

PANTHER MOUNTAIN

A CHALLENGING BUT REWARDING HIKE IN THE HEART OF THE CATSKILL MOUNTAINS

PHOENICIA

▷⋯ STARTING POINT	⋯✕ DESTINATION
GIANT LEDGE TRAILHEAD	**PANTHER MOUNTAIN**
🍺 BREWERY	🀱 HIKE TYPE
WOODSTOCK BREWING	**STRENUOUS**
🐾 DOG FRIENDLY	📅 SEASON
YES (LEASH REQUIRED)	**YEAR-ROUND**
$ FEES	🕐 DURATION
NONE	**4 HOURS**
⛰ MAP REFERENCE	↦ LENGTH
NYNJ TRAIL CONFERENCE CATSKILL CENTRAL — MAP 142	**6.5 MILES** (ROUND-TRIP)
👁 HIGHLIGHTS	〰 ELEVATION GAIN
ROCK LEDGES	**1,980 FEET**

5.5 %
ALCOHOL
CONTENT

BABY DRAGON PALE ALE

 HAZY YELLOW

 LIGHT CITRUS

 ORANGE

BITTERNESS	SWEETNESS

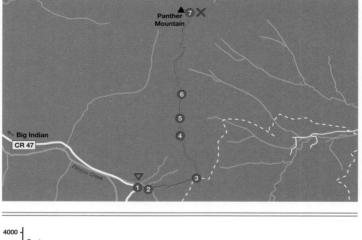

Panther Mountain

Big Indian
CR 47

Esopus Creek

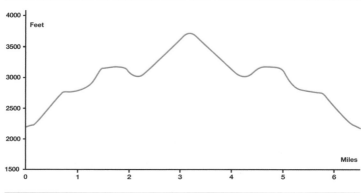

Feet

Miles

HIKE DESCRIPTION

Take in the expansive views and dramatic rock ledges on the way up Panther Mountain and you'll quickly see why this is one of the most popular hikes in the Catskills. Afterward, stop by the Woodstock Brewery, one of the area's first, which brings the spirit of an artists' retreat to the world of craft beer.

A subset of the larger Appalachian Mountains, the Catskills comprise approximately 1,000 square miles of public and private land west of the Hudson River valley, about 100 miles northwest of New York City and less than an hour's drive from the state capital in Albany. Millions of years ago, these majestic mountains rivalled today's Alps and Rockies in terms of elevation and topography. Today, the mountaintops have been somewhat eroded and flattened by time, but the Catskills still boast 35 peaks over 3,500 feet in elevation, topped by Slide Mountain at 4,180 feet. The hike to Panther Mountain is the perfect introduction to hiking in this region. It features steep, challenging inclines between more moderate sections and a few wide rock ledges that afford spectacular views to the north and east.

On weekends, the parking area fills up very quickly, so aim for an early start. The trail is well-marked and easy to follow. All the elements the Catskills have to offer are on full display over the course of this hike: steep, punchy climbs with rock ledges and stairs are interspersed with flatter sections of easily navigable terrain. There are a couple of spots where you might want to use your hands, but as with most of the hikes in the Catskills, no technical rock-climbing skill or experience is needed, nor do you need any specialized equipment—though crampons, spikes, or snowshoes may be useful in winter, depending on the conditions.

After a series of alternating climbs, you'll reach Giant Ledge, which is actually a series of rock ledges with excellent east-facing views of the

Burroughs Range (Cornell, Wittenberg, and Slide Mountains). This sub-range is named for the famous naturalist John Burroughs, who was born in this area and spent a great deal of his life exploring these mountains. (A plaque at the Slide Mountain summit commemorates Burroughs and his efforts to preserve the area he called "The Heart of the Southern Catskills.")

From Giant Ledge, the trail descends steeply to a col before ascending steadily to the top of Panther Mountain. The summit itself is unmarked and heavily wooded, with no views to speak of; however, there are impressive vistas from a large boulder just before the true summit, and from a small clearing just beyond it.

TURN-BY-TURN DIRECTIONS

1. From the parking area on the right side of Route 47, cross the road at the bend and arrive at the well-marked trailhead and a small wooden footbridge.
2. At 0.1 miles, reach the trail register (please sign in) and cross another footbridge before climbing moderately on rocky, rooted terrain.
3. At 0.8 miles, come to an intersection at the top of a short climb. Turn left and follow the blue-blazed trail toward Giant Ledge.
4. At 1.3 miles, a sign on the left directs you to a spring with potable water. You can fill your bottles here before resuming the climb steadily uphill, following the blue blazes.
5. At 1.6 miles, reach Giant Ledge, a series of rock outcroppings on the right with spectacular views to the east. Continue north on the blue blazes.
6. At 2.0 miles, the trail descends to a col before once again climbing steadily uphill.
7. At 3.0 miles, reach a large boulder on the right side of the trail; scrambling up on this will yield some nice views to the east. The unmarked summit is 0.1 miles beyond this point; another view is available just beyond the summit. Retrace your steps to return to the trailhead.

FIND THE TRAILHEAD

From Kingston/Exit 19 on the NYS Thruway, take Route 28 West for 31 miles to Big Indian. Turn left on Oliverea Road and follow it for 7.3 miles. The parking area is a pull-off on the right side of the road, just before the road bends sharply to the right, and is marked with a sign. The trailhead is just across the road.

WOODSTOCK BREWING

Despite being named for the legendary artist's colony, Woodstock Brewing is actually about 12 miles from the town of Woodstock itself (and 50 miles from Max Yasgur's farm, site of the 1969 music festival). Rick Shobin and Scott Shimomura had been homebrewing for eight years before they opened their brewery just outside of downtown Phoenicia in 2018. The spacious taproom is complemented by a large outdoor seating area and is a favorite hangout for local hikers, skiers, and fishing enthusiasts. Like many breweries in the region, the tap list is heavy on hoppy IPAs, but we suggest branching out a bit to try some of the lighter varieties, including Baby Dragon, a fruity pale ale with a bit of a hoppy bite. Pork tacos are the highlight of a solid menu with many vegan options, and coffee and wood-fired pizzas are available next door in the plaza.

LAND MANAGER

New York State Department of Environmental Conservation
1130 North Westcott Road
Schenectady, NY 12306-2014
(518) 357-2234
www.dec.ny.gov
Map: www.avenzamaps.com/maps/1487197?utm_source=affiliate&utm_
medium=affiliate_link&utm_campaign=apgar%40nynjtc.org&utm_
term=2745438757

BREWERY/RESTAURANT

Woodstock Brewing
5581 NY-28
Phoenicia, NY 12464
(518) 688-0054
www.drinkwoodstock.com
Distance from trailhead: 17 miles

WEST KILL MOUNTAIN

A CLASSIC CATSKILL PEAK FEATURING WATERFALLS AND SHORT ROCK SCRAMBLES

WEST KILL

▷⋯ STARTING POINT	⋯✕ DESTINATION
DIAMOND NOTCH FALLS PARKING AREA	**WEST KILL MOUNTAIN**
🍺 BREWERY	🀫 HIKE TYPE
WEST KILL BREWING	**STRENUOUS**
🐾 DOG FRIENDLY	📅 SEASON
YES (LEASH REQUIRED)	**YEAR-ROUND**
$ FEES	🕐 DURATION
NONE	**4 HOURS**
🗺 MAP REFERENCE	↦ LENGTH
NYNJ TRAIL CONFERENCE CATSKILL NORTHEAST — MAP 141	**6.5 MILES** (ROUND-TRIP)
🔎 HIGHLIGHTS	〰 ELEVATION GAIN
WATERFALL	**1,992 FEET**

KAATERSKILL IPA

 HAZY GOLD

CITRUS,
GRASSY

TROPICAL FRUIT,
CITRUS

BITTERNESS **SWEETNESS**

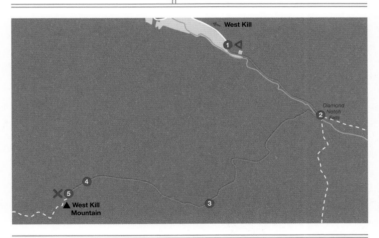

West Kill

1

Diamond
Notch
Falls
2

4
5
▲ West Kill
Mountain

3

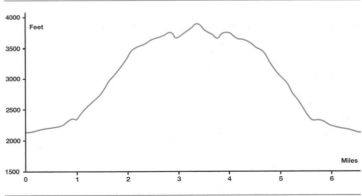

HIKE DESCRIPTION

Get a taste of the infamous Devil's Path on this vigorous hike to one of the highest peaks in the Catskills. Then, visit the family-owned West Kill brewery for a true taste of upstate NY wilderness.

The Catskill Mountains are home not only to beautiful waterfalls, rustic mountain towns, classic "Borscht Belt" summer resorts, and a variety of downhill and Nordic skiing options but also to sections of some of the state's most iconic hiking trails. The Appalachian Trail skirts the Catskills to the south and east, and several other popular thru-hikes traverse the region. The eastern terminus of the 580-mile Finger Lakes Trail is atop Slide Mountain, the highest peak in the Catskills. And 90 miles of Catskill trails, including nine 3,500-foot peaks, comprise the crux of the 360-mile Long Path from New York City to Thatcher State Park near Albany.

The Devil's Path is one of the most popular of the myriad day hikes and shorter thru-hikes that crisscross the region. Early settlers believed that the terrain was so inhospitable that the region must have been used as a retreat by the devil. The point-to-point trail, which is blazed and well-maintained, stretches 24 miles across the northern aspect of the park, with 9,000 feet of climbing spread among six different peaks separated by deep cols. While the Catskill High Peaks are relatively modest in total elevation (only a few of them make it above 4,000 feet), the steep grades and technical nature of these climbs make them extremely challenging. Unlike many hikes in the American West, Catskill trails forgo switchbacks and ease-of-use in favor of a more direct approach. Hikers on the Devil's Path must contend with steep

pitches, boulders, roots, and short rock scrambles. Experienced hikers will generally complete the Devil's Path in two or three days, and the route is a hotly contested test piece for rugged trail and mountain runners who will attempt to cover the distance in a single all-out push.

While the eastern section of the trail is more popular and more rugged, the less-traveled western Devil's Path features two classic peaks, including Hunter Mountain, the second-highest peak in the Catskill range, and several beautiful views. Our hike takes us to the summit of West Kill Mountain, the westernmost peak on the path. For the first several minutes, you'll climb gradually but steadily up a wide, rocky path, tracking the fast-flowing waters of West Kill Creek (from which the town and the mountain derive their names) on the right. Less than a mile in, you'll reach Diamond Notch Falls, a small group of waterfalls that drop over moss-covered rock under a wooden footbridge. This is a beautiful spot in all seasons. If the weather is warm, you may decide to carefully scramble down some of the adjoining rock to peer into the damp cavern behind the falls.

At the footbridge over the falls, you'll join the red-blazed Devil's Path and, following a short descent, begin the sort of difficult climb that makes this trail notorious. The next mile and a half are steep and strenuous, with a few sidehill traverses mixed in. On a few of the rocky sections you'll need to use your hands. Shortly past the 3,500-foot marker, the gradient becomes less severe, with some gentle climbing and short downhill sections leading to a false summit. The trail then descends to a col between the false and true summits before beginning the steep final climb. The mountain saves the toughest for last: the final steep rock scramble occurs just before the summit. At the top of this section, you can take a short spur trail to the left to the Buck Ridge lookout. One of the more spectacular lookouts in the Catskills, it affords sweeping views of Hunter and Southwest Hunter mountains to the east. Once you return to the main trail, the summit, marked by a small sign and rock cairn (but no view), is just a short jog away.

131

TURN-BY-TURN DIRECTIONS

1. Leave the parking area at the end of Sprucetown Road, following the blue-blazed Diamond Notch Falls Trail past the trail register at 0.2 miles.

2. At 0.8 miles, reach Diamond Notch Falls and a wooden footbridge. Cross the bridge and make an immediate right, following the red-blazed Devil's Path towards West Kill Mountain.

3. At 2.2 miles, pass a large overhanging rock on the right. Squeeze through a small crevice between two boulders and continue following the Devil's Path.

4. At 3.1 miles, following a steep rock scramble, reach the spur trail to the Buck Ridge lookout on your left. After visiting the lookout, return to the main trail.

5. At 3.3 miles, reach the summit marker. Return to the parking area via the same route.

FIND THE TRAILHEAD

From Kingston/Exit 19 on the NYS Thruway, take Route 28 West for 28 miles to Shandaken. Turn right onto NY-42 North and continue for 7.3 miles. Turn right onto Sprucetown Road and follow it for 5.7 miles to the trailhead at the end of the road.

WEST KILL BREWING

As befits a brewery nestled among some of the most challenging hiking trails in the state, West Kill Brewing embodies an ethos of "beer tastes better outdoors." The brewery collaborates with a variety of organizations to promote trail work, aids the local search-and-rescue teams, and hosts an annual fly-fishing expo. Former schoolteacher and West Kill native Mike Barcone established the brewery with his spouse Colleen Kortendick in 2017 on his family's 127-acre farm. They now grow and harvest many of the ingredients used in their beers, a varied lineup that includes lagers, pale ales, and funky farmhouse sours in addition to the signature IPA.

LAND MANAGER

New York State Department of Environmental Conservation
1130 North Westcott Road
Schenectady, NY 12306-2014
(518) 357-2234
www.dec.ny.gov
Map: www.avenzamaps.com/maps/1487196?utm_source=affiliate&utm_
medium=affiliate_link&utm_campaign=apgar%40nynjtc.org&utm_
term=4291235647

BREWERY/RESTAURANT

West Kill Brewing
2173 Sprucetown Road
West Kill, NY 12492
(518) 989-6001
www.westkillbrewing.com
Distance from trailhead: 1.4 miles

ARTISTS' WALK

ENJOY PANORAMIC VIEWS AT THE BIRTHPLACE OF A PAINTING MOVEMENT

CATSKILL

▷··· STARTING POINT	···✗ DESTINATION
THOMAS COLE HISTORIC SITE	**OLANA MANSION**
🍺 BREWERY	🎲 HIKE TYPE
CROSSROADS BREWING COMPANY	**MODERATE** 🚶
🐾 DOG FRIENDLY	📅 SEASON
YES (LEASH REQUIRED)	**YEAR-ROUND**
$ FEES	🕐 DURATION
NONE	**3 HOURS**
⛰ MAP REFERENCE	↦ LENGTH
OLANA STATE HISTORIC SITE TRAIL MAP	**6.6 MILES** (ROUND-TRIP)
🔍 HIGHLIGHTS	〰 ELEVATION GAIN
HISTORIC SITES, BRIDGE	**552 FEET**

BRICK ROW ALE

5.2 % ALCOHOL CONTENT

 AMBER

 WHEAT

 MALT, CARAMEL

BITTERNESS   SWEETNESS

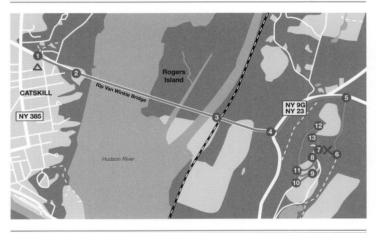

Rogers Island

CATSKILL

Rip Van Winkle Bridge

NY 385

Hudson River

NY 9G
NY 23

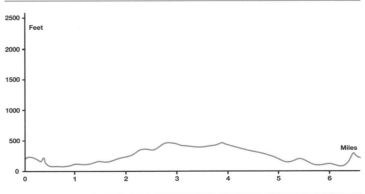

2500
2000
1500
1000
500
0

Feet

Miles

0   1   2   3   4   5   6

HIKE DESCRIPTION

Take a tour through some of the Hudson Valley's historic sites to see why the area has inspired artists for over a century. Then head to the Crossroads Brewing taproom for a casual indoor/outdoor tasting experience with a varied beer and wine selection.

We've named this hike "Artists' Walk" because it visits the homes of two influential artists: Thomas Cole, the founder of the Hudson River School of painting, and Frederic Church, Cole's star pupil and one of the most famous artists of the 19th century. Their paintings drew inspiration from their natural surroundings and focused on realistic, detail-oriented landscapes. Their work depicts not only the Hudson River Valley but also the Catskills, the Adirondacks, and the White Mountains of New England.

Begin at the Thomas Cole National Historic Site in Catskill, where you can visit the artist's immaculately curated home and view exhibitions featuring his work as well as that of his pupils and those he inspired. From here, you'll cross high over the Hudson River on the Hudson River Skywalk, a pedestrian walkway that parallels the Rip Van Winkle Bridge. From nearly 150 feet above the water, you'll be treated to lovely views to the south and a glimpse of your destination, the Olana mansion, high atop the hill ahead.

After crossing the bridge, you'll follow Route 9G uphill for about half a mile before reaching the wooded carriage roads of Olana, the 250-acre estate often described as Frederic Church's masterpiece. The painter was intimately involved in all aspects of the development of this property—from the design of the landscape and the surrounding carriage roads to the architectural plans for the 7,000-square-foot mansion. Church named the property after an ancient Persian fortress, and the building shows signs of Persian and Victorian influences. Much of its original furniture and many of its interior flourishes were acquired by the painter on his travels in the Middle East.

You'll follow a wide carriage road uphill to the main residence, which is impeccably maintained and well worth exploring. To the south, you'll see a large portion of the estate that was designed as a working farm by Church; to the east, you're treated to spectacular vistas of the Hudson, the Skywalk, and the Catskill Mountains. From the mansion, you'll follow carriage roads on a small loop around the grounds, which feature views of Mount Merino to the north. Finally, you'll retrace your steps back downhill to the Skywalk.

TURN-BY-TURN DIRECTIONS

1. Leave from the rear of the parking lot, following signs for Olana along a paved pedestrian path.

2. At 0.3 miles, cross the Rip Van Winkle Bridge using the pedestrian walkway on the right/south side of the bridge. (Public bathrooms are available on the right.)

3. At 1.3 miles, reach the east side of the bridge and pass North River Vineyards on your right; continue along the sidewalk.

4. At 1.5 miles, come to a traffic circle. Head directly across the circle to a parking area; then turn left and follow Route 9G North/ Route 23 East uphill, following signs for Olana.

5. At 2.1 miles, at the top of the hill, turn right onto a gravel path, pass through a gate and enter Olana on the North Road carriageway; continue uphill.

6. At 2.5 miles, the trail flattens out briefly as it approaches an intersection. Make a right at this intersection to continue on North Road; the trail ascends gradually, then more steeply.

7. At 2.8 miles, reach an intersection with the Ridge Road carriageway and turn left toward the parking area. Presently, cross a paved road with the Olana mansion directly ahead of you. Continue on a paved footpath that bends toward the left side of the house.

8. At 2.9 miles, from behind the main house, make a left onto the gravel New Approach (NA) carriageway, which winds downhill.

9. At 3.1 miles, the gravel path ends at the paved South Road; turn right onto the pavement and continue downhill.

10. At 3.3 miles, leave the pavement by turning right onto the gravel Ridge Road footpath.

11. At 3.4 miles, keep right at a fork in the trail.

12. At 3.7 miles, the trail makes a wide, sweeping right-hand bend, affording clear views of Mount Merino ahead, before turning back toward the mansion.

13. At 3.8 miles, make a left turn to rejoin the North Road carriageway and continue downhill. From here, retrace your steps back downhill, leaving the estate and crossing back over the river via the pedestrian path.

FIND THE TRAILHEAD

From Exit 21 of the NYS Thruway, turn left onto Main Street and follow it for 0.6 miles to Route 23. Turn left onto NY-23 East and follow it for 1.4 miles. Make a right at a traffic light onto Spring Street. The shared parking area of the Thomas Cole Historic Site and Temple Israel is immediately on the left.

CROSSROADS BREWING COMPANY

The Catskill taproom is the award-winning brewery's second location. It opened in 2017 following the success of the original brewpub in Athens, NY. The tasting room and brew tanks are housed in the former home of the *Daily Mail* newspaper in a prime location along the banks of Catskill Creek. A beautiful pedestrian bridge leads from the end of the outdoor seating area over the creek and into a local park. Inside, there are twelve rotating taps offering not only the flagship Brick Row amber ale but also a variety of lagers, IPAs, and the occasional sour. Unlike the brewery's home base, the taproom has no kitchen, but you're welcome to bring your own food, and food trucks are parked beside the patio for most of the year.

LAND MANAGER

Olana State Historic Site
5720 State Route 9G
Hudson, NY 12534
(518) 828-1872
www.olana.org
Map: www.olana.org/wp-content/uploads/2019/03/OlanaCarriage RoadMap.pdf

BREWERY/RESTAURANT

Crossroads Brewing Company
201 Water Street
Catskill, NY 12414
(518) 291-4550
www.crossroadsbrewingco.com
Distance from trailhead: 0.8 miles

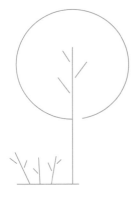

THACHER STATE PARK

AN EASY HIKE WITH IMPRESSIVE VIEWS

VOORHEESVILLE

▷⋯ STARTING POINT	⋯✗ DESTINATION
THACHER PARK NORTH TRAILHEAD	**HIGH POINT CLIFF**
🍺 BREWERY	🔲 HIKE TYPE
INDIAN LADDER FARMS CIDERY AND BREWERY	**EASY**
🐾 DOG FRIENDLY	📅 SEASON
YES (LEASH REQUIRED)	**YEAR-ROUND**
$ FEES	⏱ DURATION
NONE	**1 HOUR 45 MIN.**
⛰ MAP REFERENCE	↦ LENGTH
THACHER STATE PARK TRAIL MAP - NORTH	**4.1 MILES** (LOOP)
🔍 HIGHLIGHTS	〰 ELEVATION GAIN
CLIFFTOP VIEWS	**240 FEET**

5.0 %
ALCOHOL
CONTENT

INDIAN LAGER FARMS

 GOLD

APPLES

PINE,
HOPS

BITTERNESS	SWEETNESS

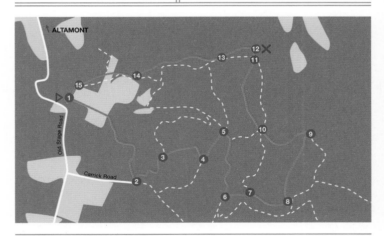

◀ ALTAMONT

Old Stage Road

Carrick Road

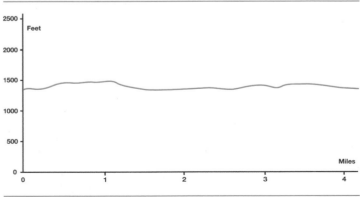

HIKE DESCRIPTION

It's almost unfair how easy this hike is considering the payoff—views of the Hudson-Mohawk Valley that stretch from the Adirondacks to the distant Green Mountains of Vermont. A visit to nearby Indian Ladder Farms is a treat for the entire family, not least those who appreciate Bavarian-influenced craft beer and cider.

Hiking is far from the only activity to be enjoyed in John Boyd Thacher State Park. Both the visitor center and the nature center offer interactive educational exhibits, and the southern end of the park features volleyball courts, playgrounds, and an adventure course with zip lines and other aerial games.

The most striking feature of Thacher State Park is the Helderberg Escarpment, a 1200-foot-high limestone cliff band that bridges the Adirondacks to the north and the Catskills to the south. The lower slopes are dotted with caves that housed Native Americans in the 17th century and provided a refuge for soldiers during the Revolutionary War. The escarpment boasts a unique geologic history and has yielded a treasure trove of fossils from the Devonian period (approximately 400 million years ago).

Starting this hike from the northwesternmost aspect of the park allows you to fully appreciate the breathtaking views from the top of the escarpment with a minimum of climbing. From the trailhead, you'll traverse a wide, open field before entering the woods on an undulating singletrack trail. After about a mile and a half, a sharp left turn points you toward Hang Glider Cliff, the first of two viewpoints on this route. You'll spend a few minutes sharing the trail with the teal-blazed Long Path, a 358-mile route starting at the George Washington Bridge. In less than a mile, you'll reach Hang Glider Cliff, where the escarpment drops away to reveal a stunning panorama of the valley below and the state capitol of Albany to the east.

After less than a mile, you'll come to an equally breathtaking view at High Point Cliff. Get there by first following a short, unmarked single-track trail, and then rejoining the Long Path for a brief jog. Either viewpoint makes for a great spot for a rest and a picnic. It's an easy ramble on a flat, wide, shaded trail back to the trailhead. For the final stretch of the hike, you'll rejoin the Long Path one last time, and will actually walk the last few steps of this epic trail, as the parking area marks the official end of the Long Path for thru-hikers.

TURN-BY-TURN DIRECTIONS

1. Leave the parking area past the metal gate and make an immediate right onto the yellow-blazed Perimeter Trail.
2. At 0.6 miles, reach a parking area at the Fred Schroeder Trailhead. Cross the parking area, heading slightly left and following the yellow markers to an information board with a trail map. Head east on the red-blazed Fred Schroeder Memorial Trail.
3. At 0.8 miles, bear right at a fork in the trail, heading south.
4. At 1.2 miles, reach an intersection with the white-blazed W3 and W4 trails. Make a right to continue on the Fred Schroeder Trail, still following the red blazes.
5. At 1.3 miles, make a right onto the white-blazed W5 Connector Trail toward Hang Glider Road.
6. At 1.6 miles, the trail ends at an intersection with the magenta-blazed Hang Glider Trail. Make a hard left and follow the Hang Glider Trail east.
7. At 1.8 miles, the teal-blazed Long Path joins from the left. Continue straight on the joint teal/magenta blazes.
8. At 2.0 miles, the Long Path turns to the right. Continue straight, following the magenta blazes toward Hang Glider Cliff.
9. At 2.4 miles, reach Hang Glider Cliff. After admiring the view, turn left onto a clear but unmarked singletrack trail (unofficially known as the Escarpment Trail) and follow this north.
10. At 2.6 miles, the trail forks. Bear left and immediately arrive at an intersection with the Long Path on the left and the Fred Schroeder Memorial Trail straight ahead. Turn right at this intersection, following the joint red and teal blazes of these two trails.
11. At 3.0 miles, the Fred Schroeder Memorial Trail and the Long Path make a left turn; bear right onto an unnamed trail marked by light blue blazes and head toward High Point Cliff.
12. At 3.1 miles, reach High Point Cliff. Make a left onto the brown-blazed High Point Road.
13. At 3.3 miles, continue straight past an unmarked trail on the left.
14. At 3.7 miles, the trail forks; bear right, continuing on High Point Road.
15. At 4.0 miles, the Long Path rejoins the trail from the left. Continue straight back to the trailhead at 4.1 miles.

FIND THE TRAILHEAD

From Albany, take I-90 West to Exit 1S for US-20/Western Avenue. Follow US-20 for 5.2 miles. Turn left onto NY-146 West and follow it for 6.6 miles as it becomes Main Street and then NY-156. Continue on NY-156 West for 1.3 miles. Make a left turn onto Old Stage Road and follow it for 0.9 miles to the parking area on your left.

INDIAN LADDER FARMS CIDERY AND BREWERY

The brewery at Indian Ladder Farms is just one of many attractions located on the grounds of this century-old facility. Visitors can pick apples, wander the trails on the property, and feed the animals in the petting zoo, and the farm hosts numerous educational and community programs throughout the year. The brewery boasts an expansive outdoor biergarten with firepits and pavilions, as well as a large indoor taproom. The twelve taps are evenly split between beer and cider. Both the beer list and the menu reveal a heavy Bavarian influence, though the fact that all the ingredients, including the hops, are grown at the farm lends a distinctly local flavor.

LAND MANAGER

John Boyd Thacher State Park
830 Thacher Park Road
Voorheesville, NY 12186
(518) 872-1237
www.parks.ny.gov/parks/thacher/details.aspx
Map: www.parks.ny.gov/documents/parks/ThacherTrailMapNorth.pdf

BREWERY/RESTAURANT

Indian Ladder Farms Cidery and Brewery
342 Altamont Road, Altamont, NY 12009
(518) 655-0108
www.indianladderfarms.com
Distance from trailhead: 7.5 miles

PEEBLES ISLAND

LOOP AROUND A HIDDEN GEM OF A PARK
JUST OUTSIDE THE STATE CAPITAL

COHOES

▷··· STARTING POINT	···✕ DESTINATION
PEEBLES ISLAND STATE PARK VISITOR CENTER	**BUTTERMILK FALLS**
🍺 BREWERY	📖 HIKE TYPE
BYE-I BREWING	**EASY** 🚶
🐾 DOG FRIENDLY	📅 SEASON
YES (LEASH REQUIRED)	**YEAR-ROUND**
$ FEES	🕐 DURATION
NONE	**1 HOUR**
⚠ MAP REFERENCE	↦ LENGTH
POSTED AT TRAILHEAD	**2.0 MILES** (LOOP)
🔍 HIGHLIGHTS	〰 ELEVATION GAIN
WATERFALLS	**23 FEET**

MIDNIGHT VEIL STOUT

11 % ALCOHOL CONTENT

 DARK BROWN

SPICY, MALT

PEPPER, CHOCOLATE

BITTERNESS

SWEETNESS

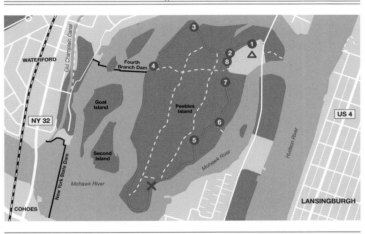

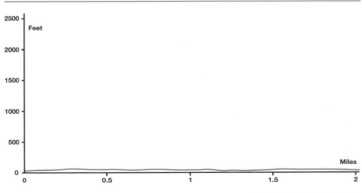

HIKE DESCRIPTION

Enjoy an easy ramble on wide paths over the rolling hills of Peebles Island State Park. Then visit the locals' hangout at Bye-i Brewing for flavorful beers in a refurbished urban setting.

Peebles Island lies at the confluence of the Mohawk and Hudson Rivers, just north of Albany. The island has a rich history. Archeologists have uncovered evidence of Native American settlements dating to the 16th century; Dutch maps from the early 17th century identify the island as the site of Menomine's Castle, a native village named for an important Mohican leader. This village overlooked a low flood plain, which made for fertile agricultural soil and provided an easy point to ford the rivers.

One of the island's first European owners was Philip Schuyler, patriarch of one of the most influential American political families in the pre-Revolutionary era. During the Revolutionary War, the island's central location lent it strategic importance, and it served as a major encampment for American troops. You can still see the remains of large earthen fortifications on the north end of the island, where the Continental soldiers prepared to make their final stand against the British army's advance south from Albany. In the mid-19th century, the island was home to workers who commuted to the nearby factories in Cohoes and Waterford. For most of the 20th century, Peebles Island was the manufacturing center of Cluett and Peabody, a leading garment manufacturer. It was purchased by the state in 1973. The remaining factory buildings now house a visitor center and the headquarters of the state's Bureau of Historic Sites and Preservation.

The trails on Peebles Island are well-marked and easy to follow, and the park is perfect for hiking, trail running, and Nordic skiing. The most popular hike is a loop around the island on the red-blazed Perimeter Trail. The trail affords excellent views of Waterford and Cohoes as well as of several waterfalls and rapids. The highlight of these is Buttermilk Falls. You'll have a nice vantage point from above these falls, which you'll come upon about three-quarters of the way through the hike on the southeastern aspect of the island. There are numerous other places along the way to stop and take in the view, complete with trailside stone benches and picnic tables. One such bench on the southern shore overlooks Van Schaick Island, another important Revolutionary War site. Cohoes Falls, the second-largest waterfall in New York, is just a mile upstream on the Mohawk River, barely out of view of the west-facing portion of the trail; if you have time, it makes for a nice side trip.

TURN-BY-TURN DIRECTIONS

1. From the parking area, head left/west on the red-blazed Perimeter Trail.
2. At 0.1 miles, turn right to stay on the Perimeter Trail.
3. At 0.2 miles, the orange-blazed Fire Road Trail intersects from the left; bear right to stay on the Perimeter Trail.
4. At 0.5 miles, continue straight on the Perimeter Trail.
5. At 1.5 miles, the yellow-blazed Deer Run Trail intersects from the left; bear right to stay on the Perimeter Trail.
6. At 1.6 miles, bear left to stay on the Perimeter Trail.
7. At 1.8 miles, continue straight on the Perimeter Trail as the blue-blazed Eagle View Trail intersects from the left.
8. At 1.9 miles, complete the loop and bear right to return to the parking lot.

FIND THE TRAILHEAD

From Albany, take I-787 North for 8.4 miles to Route 470/Ontario Street. Turn right onto Ontario Street and follow it for 0.6 miles. Turn left on Delaware Avenue/Railroad Drive and proceed for 0.9 miles. The visitor center and parking area will be on the left.

BYE-I BREWING

Opened in 2019 in a revitalizing neighborhood in downtown Cohoes, Bye-i Brewing is committed to quality and building community. The tasting room sports twelve taps with the full range of offerings on display. The brewery specializes in putting unusual twists on well-known favorites, such as brewing a pale ale with habanero peppers and adding hard-to-find Phantasm hops to its Experimental IPA. The Midnight Veil stout brings to mind a liquid S'more, with hints of graham cracker, chocolate, and marshmallow. The brewery partners with local restaurants to offer a variety of food options and hosts regular karaoke parties.

LAND MANAGER

NYS Department of Parks, Recreation, and Historic Preservation
1 Delaware Avenue North
Cohoes, NY 12047
(518) 268-2188
www.parks.ny.gov/parks/111/details.aspx
Map: www.parks.ny.gov/documents/parks/PeeblesIslandTrailMap.pdf

BREWERY/RESTAURANT

Bye-i Brewing
122 Remsen Street
Cohoes, NY 12047
(518) 244-3924
www.byeibrewing.com
Distance from trailhead: 1.8 miles

FIVE MILE TRAIL

A TOUR OF HISTORIC SARATOGA SPA STATE PARK

SARATOGA SPRINGS

▷⋯ STARTING POINT	⋯✗ DESTINATION
HALL OF SPRINGS	**ORENDA SPRING**
🍺 BREWERY	🁢 HIKE TYPE
DRUTHERS BREWING COMPANY	**EASY** 🚶
🐾 DOG FRIENDLY	📅 SEASON
YES (LEASH REQUIRED)	**YEAR-ROUND**
$ FEES	⏱ DURATION
NONE	**2 HOURS**
⌂ MAP REFERENCE	↦ LENGTH
AVAILABLE AT TRAILHEAD	**5.2 MILES** (LOOP)
🔍 HIGHLIGHTS	〰 ELEVATION GAIN
MINERAL SPRINGS, HISTORIC SITES	**151 FEET**

5.1 %
ALCOHOL CONTENT

GOLDEN RULE
BLONDE ALE

 CLEAR YELLOW

 MALT

MALT,
HINT OF PINE

BITTERNESS

5
4
3
2
1

SWEETNESS

5
4
3
2
1

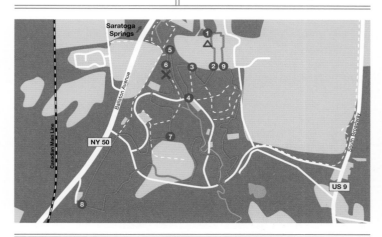

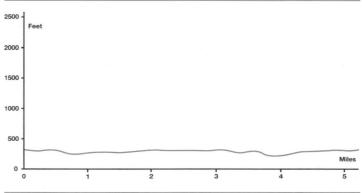

HIKE DESCRIPTION

Take a rambling tour of the diverse offerings in Saratoga Spa State Park, a National Historic Landmark. Then visit the flagship location of Druthers Brewing Company, a Capital Region mainstay in the heart of downtown Saratoga Springs.

Hundreds of years ago, the wilderness around what is today known as Saratoga Springs was a prized hunting spot of Native Americans, as animals were attracted to the area by the high mineral content of the water. The native Mohawk and Iroquois, and later European settlers in the 18th and early 19th centuries, flocked to the springs for their supposed healing powers. By the mid-1800s, Saratoga Springs had become a prime destination for wealthy vacationers and desperate so-called "invalids" alike. By the time the iconic thoroughbred racecourse opened in 1863, Saratoga was already famous as "The Queen of Spas."

The influx of visitors has only increased since a state park was established to protect the local springs from mineral-well drilling in the early 20th century. Today, the park includes mineral baths and spas, two swimming pools, a luxury hotel, and two golf courses, as well as miles of hiking trails. It's also home to a large auto museum and the Saratoga Performing Arts Center, a venue renowned around the world for its musical performances. The trails in the park are generally non-technical and easy to navigate, which attracts runners for cross-country and trail races throughout the year, and many of the trails are open for snowshoeing and Nordic skiing in the winter.

The Five Mile Trail links up several different trails and will show you much of what the park has to offer. You'll start from in front of the Hall of Springs, which is centrally located near both the auto museum and the eastern gate of the Performing Arts Center. You can pick up a trail

map from the park office, just across the lawn from the Hall of Springs, and then cross in front of the Roosevelt Baths & Spa buildings before picking up the trail. The Five Mile Trail is contiguous with several shorter trails that are marked by blazes of various colors. Since these colors will change during this hike, you should always be following the yellow, diamond-shaped markers that indicate "Five Mile Trail."

The first section of the hike follows a wide dirt path downhill to two of the park's thirteen mineral springs, "Hayes" and "Island Spouter" (the latter forms a geyser in the middle of a creek). You'll pass a monstrous mineral deposit before passing underneath the pedestrian bridge that connects the SPAC box office to the amphitheater. Nearby is Orenda Spring, where there is a spigot from which you can fill your bottle with the supposedly healing water. (It tastes horrendous.)

From here, the trail meanders through a more secluded, marshy section of the park, loops around the Peerless Pool complex following the disc golf course, drops down to parallel the southern section of Geyser Creek, and climbs back to the finish past another spring on the Ferndell Trail. The park can get busy, especially on summer and fall weekends, but the latter half of this hike is quieter and somewhat more remote, and you may well see wildlife among the reeds and marshes in this section.

TURN-BY-TURN DIRECTIONS

1. Starting from the front of the Hall of Springs, head south on a small gravel path that crosses the field in front of the park office.

2. At 0.2 miles, cross a small auto road and continue on the gravel trail straight ahead, following red discs and diamond-shaped yellow markers indicating the Five Mile Trail. For the remainder of the hike, follow these yellow markers.

3. At 0.5 miles, recross the auto road, make a left, and head downhill, keeping a chain-link fence to your right.

4. At 0.7 miles, cross a small footbridge over Geyser Creek and turn right.

5. At 1.0 miles, climb a staircase near the dam that feeds the creek. At the top of the stairs, turn left, following a paved path downhill.

6. At 1.1 miles, pass Orenda Spring on the right and bear right, leaving the paved path and following the Five Mile Trail signs onto a winding singletrack trail.

7. At 1.8 miles, bear right, following the trail counterclockwise around the pool.

8. At 2.7 miles, turn left onto a wide grassy trail and cross a small footbridge, still following the yellow markers.

9. At 4.8 miles, reach the road crossing near the Hall of Springs and the park office. Cross the road and the field to return to the start.

FIND THE TRAILHEAD

From I-87, take Exit 13N and merge onto US-9 North toward Ballston Spa. Follow US-9 North for 3 miles. Turn left onto the Avenue of the Pines to enter Saratoga Spa State Park. Continue for 1.0 miles and turn left on Hadleys Beck Road. The parking area will be immediately on the left; the Hall of Springs is straight ahead.

DRUTHERS BREWING COMPANY

Centrally located on Broadway in downtown Saratoga Springs, Druthers Brewing Company is a popular gathering place for locals and out-of-towners alike. The taproom sits back from the sidewalk, behind an impressive iron gate and the cozy beer garden. The Saratoga location opened in 2012, the first of four in the greater Albany area. The beer list combines year-round mainstays like the Golden Rule—a crisp, inventive blonde ale—and seasonal varieties like brown ales, sours, and even a brandywine ale. The menu offers a high-end take on comfort food and has several kid-friendly options; please note that dogs are not allowed.

LAND MANAGER

Saratoga Spa State Park
19 Roosevelt Drive
Saratoga Springs, NY 12866
(518) 584-2535
www.parks.ny.gov/parks/saratogaspa
Map: www.parks.ny.gov/documents/parks/SaratogaSpaSaratogaSpa-TrailMap2022.pdf

BREWERY/RESTAURANT

Druthers Brewing Company
381 Broadway
Saratoga Springs, NY 12866
(518) 306-5275
www.druthersbrewing.com
Distance from trailhead: 2.5 miles

DANIELS ROAD BEE LOOP

A SHARP CLIMB FROM A BREWERY TO VISTAS AND A POND

SARATOGA SPRINGS

▷⋯ STARTING POINT	⋯✗ DESTINATION
ARTISANAL BREW WORKS	**BEAVER POND**
🍺 BREWERY	🗺 HIKE TYPE
ARTISANAL BREW WORKS	**MODERATE** 🚶
🐾 DOG FRIENDLY	📅 SEASON
YES (LEASH REQUIRED)	**YEAR-ROUND**
$ FEES	⏲ DURATION
NONE	**2 HOURS**
⛰ MAP REFERENCE	↦ LENGTH
AVAILABLE AT BREWERY	**3.7 MILES** (LOLLIPOP)
🔍 HIGHLIGHTS	〰 ELEVATION GAIN
OVERLOOK, BEAVER POND	**319 FEET**

9.1 %
ALCOHOL
CONTENT

TRAPPIST AT THE TRACK TRIPEL

 CLEAR GOLD

MALT

MALT,
SPICE

BITTERNESS

SWEETNESS

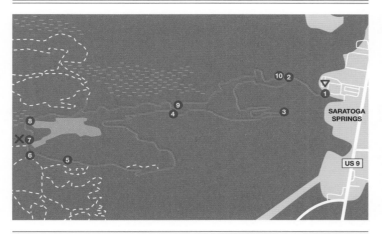

SARATOGA
SPRINGS

US 9

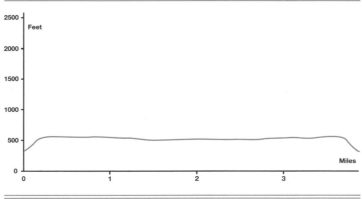

2500
2000
1500
1000
500
0

Feet

Miles

0   1   2   3

HIKE DESCRIPTION

Explore the mountain bikers' haven at Daniel's Road State Forest on a newly cut trail that begins right behind Artisanal Brew Works. Then enjoy the brewery's eclectic collection of Belgian classics, fruited sours, and candy-infused hard seltzers.

It's hard to beat a hike that starts and finishes at a brewery! This access point to the plethora of mountain biking trails at Daniel's Road State Forest opened in 2022 after an easement permitted public passage across a private property. Starting your hike from this trailhead makes the navigation a bit tricky in places, but it affords views not available elsewhere in the park, and it's certainly fun to combine an appreciation for hiking and beer in this way.

The hike starts directly behind the biergarten, following a singletrack trail marked with pink flagging tape. (There are a few green blazes, but these are inconsistent—stick to the pink flagging.) You'll start climbing almost immediately; most of the elevation gain for this hike comes in the first quarter-mile, as you ascend the eastern face of the Saratoga Fault. This

fault line provides the break in the earth's rock layers that allows the trapped water underneath to rise to the surface, producing the mineral springs for which Saratoga Springs is famous. Here, the fault provides a short but steep climb that eventually leads to an east-facing vista at a series of rock outcroppings along the top of the ridge.

Once you've reached the top of the fault line, most of the climbing is done, but the trail is rarely flat. You'll follow a twisting, narrow singletrack trail as it undulates over exposed rock slabs. About a mile into the hike, you'll begin to see some small white discs marked "SBMA." These indicate trails that are maintained by the Saratoga Mountain Bike Association, a volunteer group tasked by the Department of Environmental Conservation (DEC) with stewardship of the trails within Daniel's Road State Forest. The white blazes mark the unofficial "Bee Trail," which is your connection to the main trails that snake throughout the park.

After a couple of miles, you'll reach an intersection with the red-blazed Main Trail, which forms the spine of the trail system. This trail is wider and easier to follow as it crosses a few small bridges. Presently, the trail leads to a sizeable beaver pond, a nice spot to visit in all seasons. Track the shoreline for a bit before departing the Main Trail to complete a loop of the Bee Trail and then descend sharply back down to the brewery, where all your exertions will be richly rewarded.

TURN-BY-TURN DIRECTIONS

1. Start from the rear of the biergarten and head steeply uphill on a narrow singletrack trail, following pink flagging tape. (Maps are available inside the brewery.)

2. At 0.2 miles, reach a T-junction at the top of the hill and turn left.

3. At 0.8 miles, come to a series of lookouts on the left.

4. At 1.2 miles, continue as the markings transition from pink flagging tape to white discs, with some old, faded teal discs mixed in.

5. At 2.2 miles, another white-blazed trail joins from the left. Do not turn here; continue straight ahead, following the teal discs. The white discs will reappear shortly. Immediately afterward, the trail forks; bear right on the Bee Connector Trail.

6. At 2.3 miles, reach a large intersection and turn right on the wide, red-blazed Main Trail. The trail descends, crosses a stream on a tiny stone footbridge, and then forks; bear right, continuing to follow the red blazes.

7. At 2.4 miles, a large wooden footbridge crosses a marshy area with a beaver pond visible to the right. Continue on the trail as it bends right and follows the shoreline and then angles away to the left and uphill.

8. At 2.6 miles, make a hard right turn onto an unmarked trail, using some well-placed stones to cross a small stream.

9. At 3.0 miles, reach the fork in the trail mentioned in waypoint 6. Bear left, then make another immediate left at a second small fork. The trail is well marked with pink flags and tape in this section.

10. At 3.5 miles, reach the intersection at the top of the plateau mentioned in waypoint 2. Turn left and descend steeply downhill to the brewery.

FIND THE TRAILHEAD

From I-87, take Exit 15 for NY-50 toward Saratoga Springs/Gansevoort. Take NY 50 West for 1.1 miles and turn right onto US-9 North. Follow US-9 North for 1.8 miles. The brewery/trailhead is in a plaza on the left, behind the fire station.

ARTISANAL BREW WORKS

You may know Kurt Borchardt and Colin Quinn, the founders of Artisanal Brew Works, as the mad scientists behind Warheads Candy Ales, the notorious "extreme sours" produced in official partnership with the candy company. For the two former schoolteachers, combining candy and beer is a natural extension of their commitment to innovation and experimentation. While their unusual concoctions garner a lot of attention, the brewers cut their teeth making high-quality Belgian ales, and the best offerings in the taproom lean in this direction. Trappist at the Track, a nod both to the brewery's Belgian roots and the famous nearby racecourse, is lighter in color and smoother in body than most tripels, but it packs a punch in both flavor and strength. Kitchen development is still underway, but flatbread pizza is available most days courtesy of a partnership with a local caterer.

LAND MANAGER

NYS Department of Environmental Conservation
232 Golf Course Road
Warrensburg, NY 12885
(518) 623-1200
www.dec.ny.gov/lands/104708.html
Map: www.saratogastryders.org/resources/Documents/daniels%20
road%20trail%20map-1.pdf

BREWERY/RESTAURANT

Artisanal Brew Works
617 Maple Avenue Suite D
Saratoga Springs, NY 12866
(518) 306-4344
www.artisanalbrewworks.com
Distance from trailhead: 0 miles

MOREAU LAKE STATE PARK

VARIABLE TERRAIN PROVIDES A FUN RUN OR HIKE WITH A GREAT VIEW

GANSEVOORT

▷⋯ STARTING POINT	⋯✕ DESTINATION
MOREAU LAKE NATURE CENTER	**MOREAU OVERLOOK**
🍺 BREWERY	🔲 HIKE TYPE
DANCING GRAIN FARM BREWERY	**MODERATE**
🐾 DOG FRIENDLY	📅 SEASON
YES (LEASH REQUIRED)	**YEAR-ROUND**
$ FEES	🕐 DURATION
$10 (FREE WITH EMPIRE PASS)	**2 HOURS 30 MIN.**
⛰ MAP REFERENCE	↦ LENGTH
POSTED AT TRAILHEAD	**4.3 MILES** (LOOP)
🔍 HIGHLIGHTS	〰 ELEVATION GAIN
LAKE, VIEWPOINT	**834 FEET**

5.7 %
ALCOHOL CONTENT

HARVEST SUN SAISON

 GOLD

FRUIT

SPICY, HINT OF PEPPER

BITTERNESS	SWEETNESS
5 4 3 **2** 1	5 4 3 **2** 1

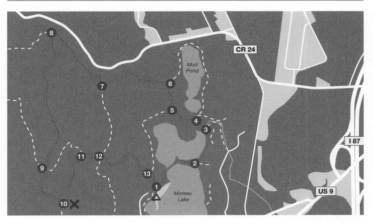

CR 24

Mud Pond

I 87

US 9

Moreau Lake

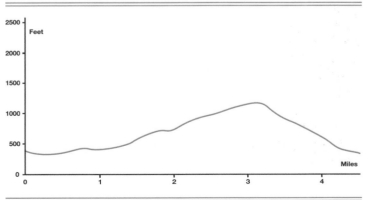

Feet

Miles

HIKE DESCRIPTION

Explore the diverse terrain surrounding Moreau Lake, a 128-acre glacial bowl that supports all manner of year-round recreation. Just a stone's throw down the road, Dancing Grain Farm Brewery offers up high-quality, sustainable beers produced on a family-owned grain farm.

Moreau Lake State Park is a bit of a hidden gem. Situated between the popular tourist destinations of Saratoga Springs and Lake George, and distinct from the well-trodden hiking terrain found in the nearby Catskills and Adirondacks, the park's 7,000 acres encompass 41 miles of hiking trails and three lakes that are open for non-motorized boating, swimming, and fishing. The terrain is varied: the trails surrounding the lakes and ponds at lower elevations are ideal for running, mountain biking, snowshoeing, and cross-country skiing, while the rockier trails along the escarpment on the western aspect of the park provide challenging climbs and descents. The park is also an important bird conservation area, as it supports several species of migratory songbirds and is a significant wintering site for many birds of prey, including bald eagles.

This hike gives you a taste of the diverse hiking opportunities this park has to offer. Start on the Nature Trail by crossing a small bridge that forms an isthmus between the northern and southern aspects of the lake. This trail leads you on a relatively smooth track along the shoreline, ideal for bird watching. After about three-quarters of a mile, you'll transition to narrow singletrack, first following the Mud Pond Trail, then the Western Ridge Trail. This section passes through thick hardwood forests, snaking through some technical terrain, over some short climbs and descents, and across several small streams. Just before

the two-mile mark, you'll reach a more remote trailhead along a small dirt road, where you'll pick up the Baker Trail. This trail climbs steeply to the top of a ridgeline before flattening to a gentler uphill grade along the ridge and leading to the aptly named Moreau Overlook.

From the overlook, the first stage of your descent back to the trailhead is fairly steep and rocky in spots; use caution in the winter when conditions can be icy on this shaded, east-facing trail. The grade becomes gentler after about half a mile, though the trail still has some steep sections and switchbacks. The trailhead is adjacent to not only the nature center but also the swimming beach, where you can take a dip if you've completed this hike on a hot summer day.

TURN-BY-TURN DIRECTIONS

1. From the map posted in front of the restrooms and nature center, head north on the Nature Trail. At the playground, make a right and cross over a wooden footbridge that divides the two sections of the lake, following the teal-blazed Nature Trail.
2. At 0.3 miles, turn left on the white-blazed Wetlands Walk.
3. At 0.5 miles, turn left to rejoin the Nature Trail.
4. At 0.6 miles, pass the orange-blazed Mud Pond Trail on the right and continue straight on the Nature Trail.
5. At 0.8 miles, turn right at the second intersection with the orange-blazed Mud Pond Trail.
6. At 1.0 miles, turn left onto the yellow-blazed Western Ridge Trail.
7. At 1.5 miles, bear right at an intersection with the red-blazed Red Oak Ridge Trail, continuing on the Western Ridge Trail.
8. At 1.9 miles, enter a small parking area. Make a hard left onto the green-blazed Baker Trail and begin climbing.
9. At 2.8 miles, reach an intersection and continue straight on the pink-blazed Ridge Run.
10. At 3.1 miles, reach the lake overlook. After admiring the view, turn left to begin descending the blue-blazed Moreau Overlook Trail.
11. At 3.5 miles, the black-blazed Old Moreau Overlook Trail joins from the left. Bear right to continue following the blue blazes.
12. At 3.7 miles, continue straight at an intersection with the Red Oak Ridge Trail, still following the blue blazes.
13. At 4.2 miles, reach the bottom of the trail and make a right turn into the parking lot. Cross the lot to return to the start at the nature center.

FIND THE TRAILHEAD

From I-87, take Exit 17S to merge onto US-9 South toward Moreau Lake State Park. After 0.3 miles, make the first right onto Old Saratoga Road and follow it for 0.7 miles to the entrance of Moreau Lake State Park on the right. After entering the park, follow the road as it bears left and clockwise around the lake for 0.8 miles to reach the parking area for the swimming beach and nature center. The hike begins at the map posted in front of the nature center.

DANICING GRAIN FARM BREWERY

A brewery was a natural extension of this second-generation family grain farm, which has been producing specialty grains for craft brewers and distillers for nearly a decade. Dancing Grain grew out of a partnership with Common Roots Brewing in nearby Glen Falls. The farm is committed to sustainably producing fresh beer in a "field-to-glass" operation. A bright, airy taproom inside a converted barn serves up a rotating selection of beers, including Harvest Sun, a slightly spicy variation on a traditional saison. Outside, the open fields provide a bucolic setting for tasting and lawn games.

LAND MANAGER

NYS Department of Parks, Recreation and Historic Preservation
605 Old Saratoga Road
Gansevoort, NY 12831
(518) 793-0511
www.parks.ny.gov/parks/150
Map: www.parks.ny.gov/documents/parks/MoreauLakeTrailMap.pdf

BREWERY/RESTAURANT

Dancing Grain Farm Brewery
180 Old West Road
Moreau, NY 12831
(518) 808-3432
www.dancinggrain.com
Distance from trailhead: 2.4 miles

PROSPECT MOUNTAIN

AN INCLINE RAILWAY BED WITH STUNNING VIEWS

LAKE GEORGE

▷⋯ STARTING POINT	⋯✗ DESTINATION
PROSPECT MOUNTAIN TRAILHEAD	**PROSPECT MOUNTAIN SUMMIT**
🍺 BREWERY	HIKE TYPE
ADIRONDACK BREWERY	**STRENUOUS**
🐾 DOG FRIENDLY	SEASON
NO	**YEAR-ROUND**
$ FEES	⏲ DURATION
NONE	**2 HOURS 30 MIN.**
⌂ MAP REFERENCE	↦ LENGTH
ADK/NATIONAL GEOGRAPHIC MAP 743	**3.1 MILES** (ROUND-TRIP)
🔍 HIGHLIGHTS	〜 ELEVATION GAIN
OLD RAILWAY MACHINERY, SUMMIT VIEWS	**1,319 FEET**

5.2 %
ALCOHOL
CONTENT

BEAR NAKED ALE

 LIGHT AMBER

 MALT

 CARAMEL,
MALT,
MILD HOPS

BITTERNESS   SWEETNESS

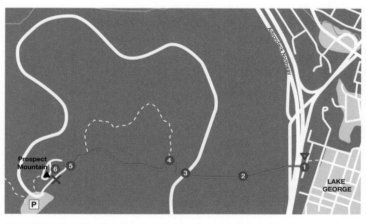

Prospect
Mountain

LAKE
GEORGE

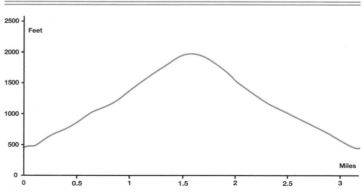

2500
2000
1500
1000
500
0

Feet

Miles

0   0.5   1   1.5   2   2.5   3

HIKE DESCRIPTION

Tackle this short but steep climb to the top of Lake George's nearest mountain to enjoy spectacular views of the popular tourist town. Then visit the Adirondack Pub and Brewery for crisp, refreshing brews in a warm, friendly atmosphere.

The village of Lake George has been a prime tourist destination for over a century. Visitors flock from all over the country to enjoy swimming, boating, and fishing on the 32-mile-long lake. There are nearly 200 islands on the lake, many of which have campsites that can be accessed by boat (camping permits and reservations are required). Situated at the southern end of the lake, the village contains a reproduction of Fort Henry, which stood on the same site in the 18th century and played a pivotal role in the French and Indian War, as depicted in the classic James Fenimore Cooper novel *The Last of the Mohicans*.

Lake George also sits in the southeastern corner of the massive Adirondack State Park and serves as a gateway to the region's myriad hikes. There are hundreds of summits within the roughly 5,000 square miles of the Adirondack Mountain range, including Mount Marcy, which at 5,344 feet is the highest mountain in New York. The summits surrounding Lake George are smaller and less severe than those in the well-known High Peaks region near Lake Placid, but still boast some of the steep, difficult trails that make the Adirondacks both notorious and beloved among hikers. The climb to the top of Prospect Mountain, whose 2,018-foot-high summit dominates the southwestern aspect of Lake George, gives hikers a perfect introduction to what hiking in the Adirondacks is all about.

The hike begins at a metal staircase leading to an enclosed pedestrian bridge that crosses the Northway (I-87) and deposits you at the base of the climb. The ascent is straightforward and easy to follow, as it roughly mirrors the course of the Otis Incline Railway, which was built in 1895 to carry passengers to the Lake House. In that day, visitors to this now-nonexistent summit resort could spend the night for the princely sum of three dollars (meals included) and enjoy the 100-mile view of the surrounding area. Remnants of what was, at the time, the world's longest incline railway are still well-preserved at the summit.

The climb is relatively easy until you reach the Prospect Mountain Veterans Memorial Highway just before the halfway point. This two-lane paved toll road is open seasonally, allowing cars access to the summit. After crossing the road, the trail becomes steeper in spots, reaching a maximum grade of about 35%. Near the summit, you'll once again cross the road as it snakes its way up toward the peak. From here, it's a short, easy climb to the top, where you can take in the breathtaking view of not only Lake George and the village, but also the Catskill and Adirondack ranges to the south and west, Vermont's Green Mountains, and the White Mountains of New Hampshire.

TURN-BY-TURN DIRECTIONS

1. From the trailhead, climb the metal staircase that leads to a pedestrian walkway over I-87. From the bottom of the stairs at the far end, begin climbing on a wide, rocky path.
2. At 0.3 miles, sign in at the trail register and continue climbing straight ahead following the red-blazed Prospect Mountain Trail.
3. At 0.6 miles, cross the paved Prospect Mountain Veterans Memorial Highway and continue uphill on the Prospect Mountain Trail.
4. At 0.7 miles, reach an intersection with a blue-blazed trail on the right; continue straight, following the red blazes.
5. At 1.3 miles, rejoin the paved Veteran's Memorial Highway. Cross the road and make a right to resume the trail, following signs indicating the summit.
6. At 1.5 miles, reach the summit of Prospect Mountain. Retrace your steps to return to the trailhead.

FIND THE TRAILHEAD

From I-87, take Exit 22 toward US-9/NY-9N/Lake George Village and merge onto NY-912Q. After 0.1 miles, turn right onto US-9 and follow it south for 0.7 miles. Turn right onto Montcalm Street and continue for 0.3 miles to the end of the road. Turn right on Cooper Street, take the first left on West Street, and then make the first left on Smith Street. The parking area is about 0.1 miles south on Smith Street, on the right side of the road, at the base of the metal staircase that leads to a pedestrian bridge over the highway.

ADIRONDACK BREWERY

Nestled in the heart of Lake George Village, less than a mile from the famed "Million Dollar Beach" at the south end of the lake, the Adirondack Pub and Brewery has been serving this bustling tourist destination for over twenty years. The brewers use locally-sourced ingredients to produce refreshing beers that can be enjoyed by the lakeside on a hot summer day. The brewpub boasts a welcoming outdoor space with large fire pits; inside, a variety of brews and pub fare are served up in a rustic lodge atmosphere. The brewery also hosts numerous events throughout the year. Lovers of spirits can stroll next door to High Peaks Distilling for award-winning whiskeys and bourbons.

LAND MANAGER

NYS Department of Environmental Conservation
1115 NYS Route 86
PO Box 296
Ray Brook, NY 12977-0296
(518) 897-1200
www.dec.ny.gov/outdoor/113217.html
Map: www.adk.org/product/map-743-lake-georgegreat-sacandaga/

BREWERY/RESTAURANT

Adirondack Pub & Brewery
33 Canada Street
Lake George, NY 12845
(518) 668-0002
www.adkbrewery.com
Distance from trailhead: 1 mile

CAT AND THOMAS MOUNTAINS

A FUN LOOP WITH TWO PEAKS AND EXCELLENT VIEWS

BOLTON LANDING

▷⋯ STARTING POINT	⋯✗ DESTINATION
CAT AND THOMAS MOUNTAINS TRAILHEAD	**CAT MOUNTAIN**
🍺 BREWERY	🀫 HIKE TYPE
BOLTON LANDING BREWING COMPANY	**STRENUOUS**
🐾 DOG FRIENDLY	📅 SEASON
YES (LEASH REQUIRED)	**YEAR-ROUND**
$ FEES	⏱ DURATION
NONE	**4 HOURS**
⛰ MAP REFERENCE	↦ LENGTH
POSTED AT TRAILHEAD	**7.2 MILES** (LOLLIPOP)
👁 HIGHLIGHTS	〰 ELEVATION GAIN
MOUNTAIN PEAKS, VIEWS, POND	**1,372 FEET**

5.8 %
ALCOHOL CONTENT

MORNING PITCH
BLONDE ALE

 HAZY ORANGE

 FRUITY

 WHEAT,
HINT OF BLUEBERRIES

BITTERNESS	SWEETNESS
5	5
4	4
3	3
2	2
1	1

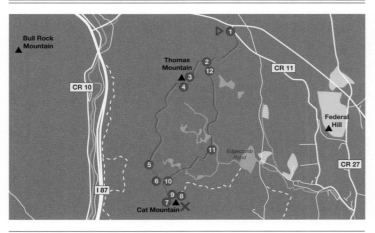

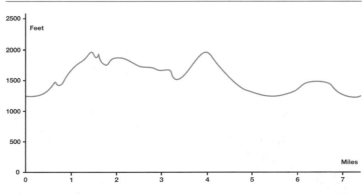

HIKE DESCRIPTION

This invigorating hike is an enjoyable romp illustrative of the varied terrain you'll find in the southern Adirondacks. Bolton Landing Brewing Company offers a friendly spot for flavorful brews in the heart of a charming lakeside village.

Situated above the town of Bolton Landing on the western shore of Lake George, the Cat and Thomas Mountains Preserve is part of the Lake George Wild Forest, a 72,000-acre section of the Adirondack Forest Preserve. Just fifteen miles north of Lake George Village, Bolton Landing offers visitors many of the same appealing activities—swimming, fishing, boating, and hiking chief among them—in a somewhat more languorous setting. The town's best-known attraction is the Sagamore, a luxury resort on nearby Green Island that has been pampering well-heeled tourists for 140 years.

At just about 2,000 feet in elevation, Cat and Thomas Mountains are relatively small compared to the summits found in the nearby High Peaks region, which makes this hike an easier introduction to Adirondack hiking, and more amenable to attempting in the winter, when a trip to the High Peaks would require at least crampons and snowshoes. You'll begin at the small parking area off Valley Woods Road, following the trail toward Thomas Mountain. This wide, rocky path heads south, climbing gradually with some short steep sections before reaching an intersection with the Richard Hayes Phillips Trail. Follow this trail more sharply uphill for less than a mile to the summit of Thomas Mountain, which opens on a nice south-facing view of Cat Mountain with some glimpses of Lake George.

From the Thomas Mountain summit, the trail descends steeply over some rocky terrain that requires you to use your hands in spots, before flattening a bit as it enters the valley between the two peaks. The next two miles are an enchanting hike along a winding singletrack path featuring short scrambles over rocky outcroppings and small stream crossings. Upon reaching the Cat Mountain Trail, you'll have a steeper climb of about half a mile to the summit. The view from the top of Cat Mountain is a breathtaking 270-degree vista dominated by Lake George to the south and east. You'll also be able to spot nearby Trout Lake and Edgecomb Pond and several southern Adirondack peaks. The Cat Mountain Trail provides a somewhat easier return route and has the added benefit of passing a lovely beaver pond, though this section of the trail can be wet and muddy in the spring.

TURN-BY-TURN DIRECTIONS

1. From the parking area, pass through the yellow metal gate and head south past the trail register on the blue-blazed Thomas Mountain Trail.
2. At 0.8 miles, bear right onto the yellow-blazed Richard Hayes Phillips Trail, following signs toward Thomas Mountain.
3. At 1.4 miles, reach the top of a steep climb. Ignore the inviting but unmarked trail straight ahead and instead bear left and continue to follow the yellow blazes.
4. At 1.5 miles, reach the overlook at the summit of Thomas Mountain. Continue downhill past the summit on the yellow-blazed trail heading west.
5. At 3.1 miles, a short spur trail to the right leads to a view of the High Peaks region to the west. After admiring this view, return to the main trail.

6. At 3.4 miles, make a right onto the blue-blazed Cat Mountain Trail.
7. At 3.7 miles, the trail turns right and flattens out briefly before the summit push.
8. At 3.8 miles, reach the summit of Cat Mountain. Retrace your steps downhill on the Cat Mountain Trail.
9. At 4.0 miles, turn left, continuing to follow the blue blazes downhill.
10. At 4.3 miles, pass the intersection with the yellow-blazed trail on the left and continue straight downhill on the Cat Mountain Trail.
11. At 5.2 miles, reach an intersection with a red-blazed trail on the right. Turn left, continuing to follow the blue-blazed Cat Mountain Trail. Presently, the trail passes a large unnamed beaver pond on the left.
12. At 6.5 miles, arrive at an intersection with the yellow-blazed Richard Hayes Phillips Trail on the left (see step 2 above), completing the large loop. Continue straight on the blue-blazed Thomas Mountain Trail to return to the trailhead.

FIND THE TRAILHEAD

From I-87, take Exit 24 toward Bolton Landing/Riverbank Road. Make a right off the exit ramp and head east for 2.0 miles before making a right turn onto Valley Woods Road. The trailhead parking area is immediately on the right and is well-marked with a large sign.

BOLTON LANDING BREWING COMPANY

Located in the heart of the small downtown district, Bolton Landing Brewing Company is a favorite hangout for both locals and visitors to the area. Founded in 2017, the brewery boasts a well-appointed taproom with high, open ceilings and a glass-encased tank room. A sizeable outdoor patio features shuffleboard and cornhole in the summer, and enclosed warming pods and fire pits in the winter. Ten rotating taps highlight inventive takes on a variety of beer styles; the Morning Pitch blonde ale comes with whole blueberries sprinkled on top. The menu offers an upscale take on usual pub fare, under the direction of a former Sagamore chef, Jonny Moulton.

LAND MANAGER

NYS Department of Environmental Conservation
232 Golf Course Road
PO Box 220
Warrensburg, NY 12885
(518) 623-1200
www.dec.ny.gov/lands/53165.html
Map: www.dec.ny.gov/docs/lands_forests_pdf/maplgwfnorth.pdf

BREWERY/RESTAURANT

Bolton Landing Brewing Company
4933 Lake Shore Drive
Bolton Landing, NY 12814
(518) 644-2739
www.boltonlandingbrewing.com
Distance from trailhead: 4.6 miles

MARCY DAM AND INDIAN FALLS

A CHALLENGING HIKE IN THE HEART OF THE ADIRONDACK HIGH PEAKS

LAKE PLACID

▷··· STARTING POINT	···✗ DESTINATION
ADIRONDACK LOJ AND HIGH PEAKS INFORMATION CENTER	**INDIAN FALLS**
🍺 BREWERY	HIKE TYPE
LAKE PLACID PUB & BREWERY	**STRENUOUS**
🐾 DOG FRIENDLY	📅 SEASON
YES (LEASH REQUIRED)	**YEAR-ROUND**
$ FEES	🕐 DURATION
$15	**5 HOURS 30 MIN.**
⛰ MAP REFERENCE	⊢ LENGTH
POSTED AT TRAILHEAD	**9.9 MILES** (LOLLIPOP)
🔍 HIGHLIGHTS	〰 ELEVATION GAIN
WATERFALL, MOUNTAIN VIEWS	**1,689 FEET**

7.0 %
ALCOHOL CONTENT

UBU ALE

DARK REDDISH-BROWN

MALT

EARTHY,
FRUIT,
HINT OF TOFFEE

BITTERNESS   SWEETNESS

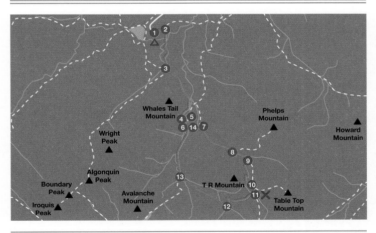

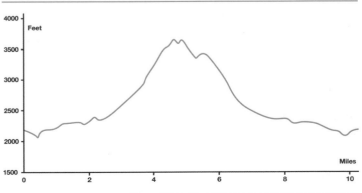

HIKE DESCRIPTION

Just outside of historic Lake Placid, hike through the pine trees to Marcy Dam and Indian Falls, in the heart of the Adirondack's High Peaks. Then, sample an Ubu Ale at the Lake Placid Pub & Brewery, twice named the best brewery in New York State.

The town of Lake Placid is the closest approximation to a European ski village in the state. This charming village has twice hosted the Winter Olympics and was the site of the US hockey team's famous "Miracle on Ice" victory over the unbeatable Soviets in 1980. Lake Placid remains a training hub for Olympic hopefuls in skating, skiing, bobsled, luge, and skeleton. Visitors flock to Placid year-round to ski the Olympic slopes at Whiteface Mountain, ride on the original bobsled track from the 1932 Games, and skate on the outdoor speed-skating oval. In the summertime, hard-core athletes descend on the town for the Ironman triathlon, which starts in the middle of town with a swim in Mirror Lake.

Its location in the midst of the Adirondack High Peaks region makes Lake Placid a prime destination for hikers. The Adirondack Loj, which provides a variety of rustic accommodations, and the trail to Marcy

Dam serve as a gateway through which hikers can access Phelps Mountain, Table Top Mountain, Wrights Peak, Algonquin Peak, and the Great Range Traverse, which includes Mount Marcy, New York's highest peak. The route to Marcy Dam along the Van Hoevenberg Trail is relatively flat and easy to follow. The wooden dam, originally built in the 1930s, was partially destroyed by Hurricane Irene in 2011 and (in keeping with modern conservation principles) will not be rebuilt. You can see the remnants of the dam on either side of Marcy Brook. Following the storm, the trail was rerouted downstream and now crosses the brook over a wooden footbridge. The area around Marcy Dam is an extremely popular site for camping, with several campsites and lean-tos maintained by the DEC.

From Marcy Dam, you'll make a large clockwise loop to visit Indian Falls, roughly circumnavigating the lower slopes of TR Mountain (named after President Teddy Roosevelt, the former governor of New York and a frequent adventurer in the Adirondacks). This section of the trail is considerably more difficult, as the terrain becomes much more rugged and the hike to the falls involves a significant amount of climbing. You'll pass through stands of oak, ash, and pine. Wildlife sightings are common here, including of deer, foxes, beavers, and black bears. Leaving the falls, the loop returns to Marcy Dam, from which it's an easy ramble back to the parking area.

TURN-BY-TURN DIRECTIONS

1. From the High Peaks Information Center, cross the parking lot to sign in at the trail register and proceed on the blue-blazed Van Hoevenberg Trail.
2. At 0.1 miles, continue straight across the XC Ski Trail.
3. At 1.0 miles, make a left and continue on the Van Hoevenberg Trail toward Marcy Dam.
4. At 2.2 miles, reach the remnants of Marcy Dam. Follow the trail left and downhill.
5. At 2.3 miles, cross the footbridge over Marcy Brook, then make an immediate right at the signs for Phelps Mountain and Indian Falls, continuing to follow the blue blazes.
6. At 2.4 miles, reach the Marcy Dam trail register. Turn left to continue on the Van Hoevenberg Trail, following signs toward Indian Falls.
7. At 2.7 miles, cross Phelps Brook and continue on the Van Hoevenberg Trail.
8. At 3.4 miles, bear right at a fork to continue on the Van Hoevenberg Trail.
9. At 3.7 miles, bear right to continue uphill on the Van Hoevenberg Trail.
10. At 4.4 miles, continue straight, passing the trail to Table Top on the left.
11. At 4.5 miles, cross a stream and then make a right onto a short spur trail to Indian Falls. Return to the main trail and head right. Arriving at a large intersection, turn right onto the yellow-blazed Lake Arnold Crossover Trail.
12. At 5.4 miles, turn right onto the blue-blazed Lake Arnold Trail, following signs toward Marcy Dam.
13. At 6.5 miles, turn right on the yellow-blazed Avalanche Pass Trail.
14. At 7.5 miles, bear left to follow signs to the Adirondack Loj and arrive back at the Marcy Dam trail register. Retrace your steps on the Van Hoevenberg Trail to return to the parking lot.

FIND THE TRAILHEAD

From the Northway/I-87, take Exit 30 for US-9 toward NY-73/Keene Valley. Follow US-9 North for 2.2 miles. Bear left onto NY-73 West and follow it for 24 miles. Turn left onto Adirondack Loj Road and follow it for 4.7 miles to its end at the Adirondack Loj and High Peaks Information Center.

LAKE PLACID PUB & BREWERY

At the south end of Mirror Lake, across the street from a public beach and just a short walk from the historic Olympic venues and museum, the Lake Placid Pub & Brewery is a can't-miss attraction for visitors to one of the Adirondack's premier tourist towns. You'll find hikers, skiers, skaters, climbers, and Olympic hopefuls at the downstairs bar, enjoying the food in the two-storey brewpub or a pint on the rooftop deck overlooking the lake. Perhaps no brewery is more closely associated with its flagship beer as the LPP&B is with Ubu Ale, a dark, full-bodied English Strong Ale that has garnered multiple golds at the World Beer Awards. All of the beer is brewed on-site (the commercial-scale brewing and distribution takes place at FX Matt Brewing in Utica). In 2016, the brewery's owners opened a second location in Lake Placid, the Big Slide Brewery & Public House, and plans are in the works for a third location in nearby Saranac Lake.

LAND MANAGER

NYS Department of Environmental Conservation
625 Broadway
Albany, NY 12233
(518) 402-8545
www.dec.ny.gov/outdoor/9198.html#High_Peaks
Map: www.adk.org/product/high-peaks-adirondack-trail-map/

BREWERY/RESTAURANT

Lake Placid Pub & Brewery
813 Mirror Lake Drive
Lake Placid, NY 12946
(518) 523-3813
www.ubuale.com
Distance from trailhead: 8.3 miles

STAR FIELD LOOP

ROLLING HILLS LEADING TO AN IDYLLIC OASIS ON OLD FARMLAND

COOPERSTOWN

▷⋯ STARTING POINT	⋯✗ DESTINATION
CHICKEN FARM HILL ROAD	**STAR FIELD**
🍺 BREWERY	🔳 HIKE TYPE
BREWERY OMMEGANG	**MODERATE** 🥾
🐾 DOG FRIENDLY	📅 SEASON
YES (LEASH REQUIRED)	**APRIL—NOVEMBER**
$ FEES	🕐 DURATION
NONE	**2 HOURS**
⛰ MAP REFERENCE	↦ LENGTH
STAR FIELD TRAIL ON ALLTRAILS.COM	**4.2 MILES** (LOLLIPOP)
🔍 HIGHLIGHTS	〰 ELEVATION GAIN
LAKE VIEWS	**387 FEET**

7.7 %
ALCOHOL CONTENT

HENNEPIN FARMHOUSE SAISON

GOLD

MILD FRUIT

SMOOTH,
MILD HOPS

BITTERNESS	SWEETNESS
5	5
4	4
3	3
2	2
1	1

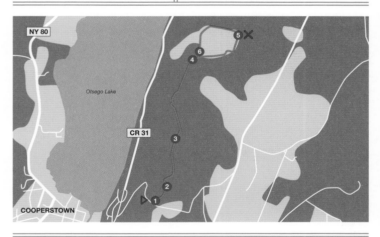

NY 80

Otsego Lake

CR 31

COOPERSTOWN

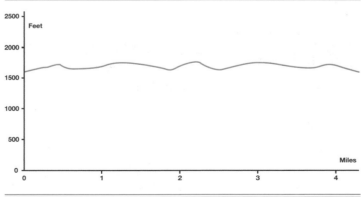

2500
Feet
2000
1500
1000
500
0
0   1   2   3   4   Miles

HIKE DESCRIPTION

Follow a two-hundred-year-old trail through the woods to a field overlooking Lake Otsego. Then visit Brewery Ommegang, one of the oldest breweries in the state, for famous Belgian-style ales, camping, live music, and more.

The village of Cooperstown rests at the southern tip of Otsego Lake and is home to the National Baseball Hall of Fame, the Farmers' Museum, and the Glimmerglass Festival—the second-largest opera festival in the US, which runs for four weeks every summer. The village is a premiere tourist destination, known for its many museums, its historic downtown district, its wealth of outdoor activities, and its well-regarded restaurants and hotels.

Star Field overlooks the lake from its perch atop the Middlefield Hills, just east of town. The field and the trail leading to it once made up the Chalet Farm. In the early 19th century, it was owned by James Fenimore Cooper—son of the town's founder William Cooper and author of the classic novel *Last of the Mohicans*. The property was later purchased by the Clark family, one of the original patent-holders of the Singer sewing machine. The Clarks remain among the most influential families in central New York, where they support a wide variety of community and artistic initiatives. They were among the founding partners of the Baseball Hall of Fame, and the nearby Clark Sports Center is the site of the Hall's induction ceremony every summer.

The trailhead is on the west side of Chicken Farm Hill Road, across from a nondescript parking area that is only large enough for a few cars. Note that the road is closed in the winter. You'll skirt some private

property on the left for the first few minutes of the hike before you enter the woods on an old bridle path. The trail soon narrows and undulates through some lovely pine and hemlock stands. There are no blazes, but the route is easy to follow. A few small side trails are marked with cairns. Low-lying areas can get a bit muddy, but these are easy to skirt. The combination of generally good footing and moderate uphill and downhill grades make this an ideal route for trail running.

After about a mile and a half, you'll reach Star Field, a wide grassy expanse with a mowed path around its perimeter. Directly ahead there is a small pond that forms an oasis in the lower part of the field. The perimeter loop is about a mile long and undulates pleasantly. At the far northeast corner of the field, a side trail on the right is marked with a cairn; this leads to a small network of interconnecting trails, though they do not progress terribly far. Otsego Lake comes into view as you approach the western edge of the field, and you can catch glimpses of downtown Cooperstown and the Otesaga, a famous lakeside luxury resort. After completing the loop around the field, it's easy to retrace your steps back to the trailhead.

TURN-BY-TURN DIRECTIONS

1. Cross the road from the small parking area and begin by hiking west on the trail toward Star Field.
2. At 0.2 miles, the trail forks; bear left.
3. At 0.7 miles, continue straight ahead, ignoring a small spur trail to the right.
4. At 1.5 miles, arrive at Star Field. Turn right on the mowed path to proceed counterclockwise around the field.
5. At 2.1 miles, continue past a side trail on the right marked with a cairn.
6. At 2.6 miles, finish the loop around Star Field and retrace your steps to arrive back at the trailhead.

FIND THE TRAILHEAD

From I-88, take Exit 24 toward US-20/NY-7/Duanesburg. Turn left onto Duanseburgh Road and follow it for 1.0 miles. Bear right onto US-20 West and continue for 29 miles. Turn left onto County Road 34 A and follow it for 0.5 miles until it becomes County Road 54. Continue on County Road 54 for 2.9 miles. Turn left onto NY-166 South and follow it for 2.2 miles. Turn right onto County Highway 33 and follow it for 9.5 miles; then make a right turn onto Kraham Road. After 0.3 miles, Kraham Road becomes Chicken Farm Hill Road. The trailhead is 0.6 miles further along, on the right side of the road. A small parking area, large enough for perhaps three cars, is on the left, directly across from the trailhead.

BREWERY OMMEGANG

Established in 1997 on the site of a former hop farm, Brewery Ommegang quickly became one of the largest and best-regarded breweries
in the state, and one of the premiere crafters of Belgian beers in the
US. The Belgian brewery Duvel was among the original investors in
Ommegang and today owns the controlling interest, but all beer is still
produced on-site. You can enjoy an impressive array of Belgian beers
and eats in a high-end taproom that opens onto a large outdoor cov-
ered patio. All of the varieties are worth trying, but Hennepin is an
absolute must-have; along with Boulevard's Tank 7, it is considered
one of the best American examples of a farmhouse saison. The brewery has partnered with Cornell University to promote local hop farming
and produce beers made exclusively with NY state hops. The 140-acre
farm, home to the production and distribution arms of the brewery,
also contains an amphitheater for live music and a nine-hole disc-golf
course and offers places to camp during festivals and events. The
brewery even sponsors an amateur cycling team.

LAND MANAGER

The Clark Foundation
19 Main Street
Cooperstown, NY 13326
(607) 547-2561
www.clarkscholarship.org
Map: www.alltrails.com/trail/us/new-york/star-field-trail

BREWERY/RESTAURANT

Brewery Ommegang
656 County Highway 33
Cooperstown, NY 13326
(607) 286-4144
www.ommegang.com
Distance from trailhead: 6.6 miles

GREEN LAKES LOOP

AN EASY HIKE IN A PICTURESQUE SETTING

MANLIUS

▷··· STARTING POINT	···✗ DESTINATION
GREEN LAKE ENVIRONMENTAL EDUCATION CENTER	**ROUND LAKE**
🍺 BREWERY	▦ HIKE TYPE
BURIED ACORN BREWING COMPANY	**EASY** 🚶
🐾 DOG FRIENDLY	📅 SEASON
YES (LEASH REQUIRED)	**YEAR-ROUND**
$ FEES	🕐 DURATION
$10 (FREE WITH EMPIRE PASS)	**1 HOUR**
⛰ MAP REFERENCE	↦ LENGTH
GREEN LAKES STATE PARK TRAIL MAP	**2.9 MILES** (LOOP)
🔍 HIGHLIGHTS	〜 ELEVATION GAIN
GLACIAL LAKES	**38 FEET**

5.5 %
ALCOHOL
CONTENT

GHOSTER BLANC SOUR

 LIGHT COPPER

 FUNKY

APPLE,
PASSIONFRUIT,
LEMON ZEST

BITTERNESS

SWEETNESS

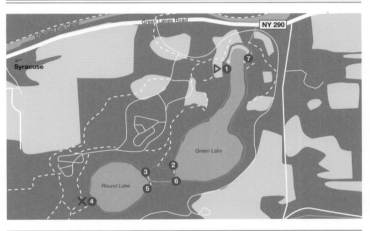

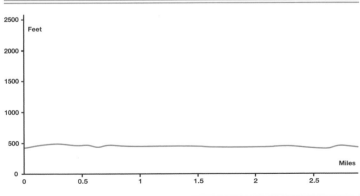

HIKE DESCRIPTION

Stroll along well-maintained trails through old-growth forests around the blue-green waters of Green Lake and Round Lake. At Buried Acorn Brewing Company, challenge your palate with a wide selection of funky sours and experimental ales.

Much of the topography and geology of western New York was formed about 10,000 years ago at the end of the last ice age. The northward retreat of the glaciers left deep canyons, gorges, cliffs, fissures, and lakes that lend the area much of its natural beauty. The deep pools at Green Lakes State Park are no exception. The twin lakes you'll see on this hike are fascinating in their origins and ecology. Both are unexpectedly deep for their size, which implies that they likely originated as the "plunge pools" of enormous waterfalls during the glacial melt.

The name shared by the park and its largest lake is a reference to the latter's distinctive green-blue color. This is the result of "whiting," a phenomenon caused by high concentrations of sulfur, calcium, and magnesium. The crystallization of these minerals, when refracted by the sun, creates the greenish color of the water. These calcite precipitates settle throughout the year, covering much of the lake floor and creating microecosystems similar to saltwater reefs.

The entire ecosystem of Green and Round Lakes is of particular interest to limnologists, as both are examples of meromictic lakes. These rare lakes (there are only four others in all of New York State) are notable in that there is no seasonal mixing of the layers of water. This creates an oxygen-poor environment in the lower layers that mimics the deep ocean. The lack of mixing also preserves the lowest sedimentary layers, where the fossil record has lain undisturbed since the lakes were formed. Because of this unique ecosystem, these lakes are among the most studied in the world. This sensitive environment also means that outside boats are not allowed; rowboats and kayaks used only within the park are available for rent during the summer months.

The trails around the lakes are mostly wide, flat, and well-graded: perfect not only for hiking but also for biking, trail running, and Nordic skiing. You'll pass intersections for different trails which lead up to "the Serengeti," a wide, grassy plain above the lake gorge on the western aspect of the park. To the north and west, the park is bordered by the Erie Canal, a 200-year-old, 360-mile manmade waterway connecting the Great Lakes and the Atlantic Ocean. Winding around Round Lake, you'll pass through old-growth stands of tulip trees, sugar maples, hemlock, beech, and cedar. Along the southern shore of Green Lake, you'll encounter Dead Man's Point, a living reef formed by thousands of years of deposition of calcium carbonate precipitate. The reef is of particular interest to botanists due to its rare aquatic mosses and sponges. In addition to the swimming beach that you'll pass toward the end of the loop, the park also contains campsites, a disc golf course, and an 18-hole golf course designed by famed course architect Robert Trent Jones.

TURN-BY-TURN DIRECTIONS

1. Starting from the Environmental Education Center, head right/ south on the Green Lake Trail.
2. At 0.6 miles, the trail forks; bear right, away from the lake.
3. At 0.8 miles, bear right on the Round Lake Trail, heading counterclockwise around Round Lake.
4. At 1.2 miles, pass the brown-blazed Brookside Trail on the right and continue straight on the Round Lake Trail.
5. At 1.6 miles, pass the small pumphouse on the right, then bear right as the trail forks, leaving Round Lake.
6. At 1.7 miles, bear right and rejoin the Green Lake Trail.
7. At 2.7 miles, pass the swimming beach on the left and the bathhouse on the right. Continue counterclockwise around Green Lake, returning to the start at 2.9 miles.

FIND THE TRAILHEAD

From I-90 (NYS Thruway), take Exit 34A for I-481 South. Follow I-481 South for 2.5 miles and take Exit 5E toward Kirkville Road. Follow Kirkville Road for 1.6 miles. Turn right onto Fremont Road and follow it for 1.2 miles. Turn left onto NY-290 East and follow for 1.7 miles; then turn left to continue on NY-290 East for another 1.6 miles. Make a right turn to enter the park at Green Lakes Park Drive. The parking area is 0.4 miles down this road on your right.

BURIED ACORN BREWING COMPANY

Located on the banks of Onondaga Creek in Syracuse, Buried Acorn Brewing Company is renowned for its wide selection of barrel-aged sours and farmhouse ales. Both the main brewery in the lakefront district and the downtown taproom feature a selection of up to thirty beers, ranging from mixed-fermentation wild ales to high-ABV imperial stouts. Ghoster Blanc is fermented with a mix of Brettanomyces and Sauvignon Blanc yeasts and then aged in red-wine barrels, giving it a zesty, fruity funkiness. There is a spirit of irreverent experimentation in the brewing, which is exemplified by some hilariously named beers such as "Satan's Little Helper" (a sour stout), "Little Timmy's Slingshot" (a pilsner brewed with Brettanomyces), and "1000 Tiny Michael Jacksons Breakdancing in Your Mouth" (a blonde ale). Both kitchens offer soups, salads, sandwiches, and flatbread pizza.

LAND MANAGER

NYS Department of Parks, Recreation, and Historic Preservation
7900 Green Lakes Road
Fayetteville, NY 13066
(315) 637-6111
www.parks.ny.gov/parks/172/details.aspx
Map: www.parks.ny.gov/documents/parks/GreenLakesTrailMap.pdf

BREWERY/RESTAURANT

Buried Acorn Brewing Company
881 Van Rensselaer Street
Syracuse, NY 13204
(315) 552-1499
www.buriedacorn.com
Distance from trailhead: 12.1 miles

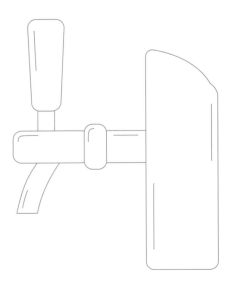

LETCHWORTH STATE PARK

STUNNING VIEWS FROM THE RIM OF A DEEP CANYON

CASTILE

▷⋯ STARTING POINT	⋯✗ DESTINATION
ST. HELENA PICNIC AREA	**LOWER FALLS OVERLOOK**
🍺 BREWERY	🗺 HIKE TYPE
SILVER LAKE BREWING PROJECT	**MODERATE** 🚶
🐾 DOG FRIENDLY	📅 SEASON
YES (LEASH REQUIRED)	**YEAR-ROUND**
$ FEES	🕐 DURATION
$10 (FREE WITH EMPIRE PASS)	**4 HOURS**
⛰ MAP REFERENCE	↦ LENGTH
LETCHWORTH PARK MAP	**10.1 MILES** (ROUND-TRIP)
🔍 HIGHLIGHTS	〜 ELEVATION GAIN
WATERFALLS	**1,049 FEET**

5.5%
ALCOHOL CONTENT

THE STANDARD CREAM ALE

 CLOUDY YELLOW

MALT

CREAMY, WHEAT

BITTERNESS	SWEETNESS
5	5
4	4
3	3
2	2
1	1

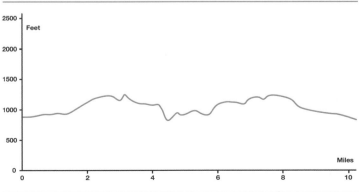

CR 55

CR 38

Castile

Genesee River

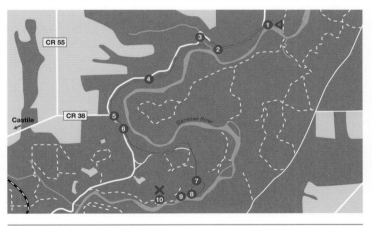

Feet

Miles

HIKE DESCRIPTION

Admire the breathtaking views as you hike along the rim of the "Grand Canyon of the East." Then visit the nearby town of Perry, where the Silver Lake Brewing Project offers up rustic farmhouse beer styles with an experimental spirit.

As it flows from Pennsylvania's Allegheny Mountains north to Rochester and Lake Ontario, the Genessee River carves a deep canyon through the gorges of Letchworth State Park. The cliff walls rise as high as 600 feet above the river, providing magnificent vistas of the surrounding forests and the three massive waterfalls within the park. There are myriad ways to explore this majestic park: by foot, on the over 60 miles of hiking trails; on the water, by kayaking or whitewater rafting; or by air, as hot air balloons ferry visitors through the canyon almost daily.

The Gorge Trail, along the canyon's western rim, provides an excellent vantage point from which to view the river and canyon year-round. The singletrack trail winds through the forest on the rim, with short, steep climbs and descents mixed with flat grassy interludes that open onto overlooks. After about a mile, you'll cross over Wolf Creek, named for the timber wolves that made their dens in the cliffs in the 19th century. Just past the bridge, you can look back and admire the first of three cascading waterfalls fed by Wolf Creek, nicknamed Wide Expanse.

After passing the park entrance, continue north along the trail. The park will become more populated, and you'll see campgrounds, pavilions, and playgrounds. The trail briefly joins the park road leading to Lower Falls Restaurant. When the trail leaves the road again, you'll follow it for about half a mile, climbing a series of staircases, before reaching the top of a staircase that descends to Lower Falls. This steep descent is closed in winter but when open leads to a nice view of Lower Falls and a footbridge you can cross to get to the eastern side of the river. Continuing past these stairs, you'll reach Lower Falls Overlook in just a quarter-mile. You can retrace your steps to complete the hike, or, if the weather permits and the trails are open, explore further south to see Middle and Upper Falls further upstream.

TURN-BY-TURN DIRECTIONS

1. The trail begins at the south end of the St. Helena Picnic Shelter parking lot. Follow the pink-blazed Gorge Trail (noted as trail number 1 on some maps) south, with the rim of the gorge to your left.
2. At 0.7 miles, reach the Tea Table Picnic Area. There is a viewpoint on the left, just beyond the parking lot. Continue on the Gorge Trail.
3. At 1.0 miles, cross a footbridge over Wolf Creek and ascend a stone staircase, remaining on the Gorge Trail.
4. At 2.0 miles, reach the Great Bend Overlook. Continue on the Gorge Trail.
5. At 2.7 miles, pass the park entrance on the right. Continue on the Gorge Trail.
6. At 3.0 miles, reach the Archery Field Overlook. Continue on the Gorge Trail.
7. At 4.4 miles, join the auto road downhill as it bears left toward Lower Falls Restaurant. Cross the road and bear right to remain on the pink-blazed Gorge Trail.
8. At 4.7 miles, bear right at a junction to continue on the Gorge Trail. Ascend a series of stone staircases, passing a playground on the right.
9. At 4.8 miles, continue straight past the staircase on the left (closed in winter), following signs for the Lower Falls Overlook.
10. At 5.0 miles, reach the Lower Falls Overlook. Retrace your steps to return to the trailhead.

FIND THE TRAILHEAD

From Rochester, take I-490 West for 17 miles to Exit 1. Take Exit 1 for NY-19 South and continue for 12 miles. Turn left onto NY-63 South and follow it for 1.0 miles. Make a right onto NY-246 South and follow it for 10.5 miles to NY-39 West. Turn right onto NY-39 West and continue for 6.3 miles. Turn left onto East Park Road, which after 0.8 miles becomes Glen Iris Road, and continue on Glen Iris Road for 1.5 miles. Turn left onto Denton Corners Road to enter Letchworth State Park. Past the park entrance, turn left onto Park Road and drive 2.6 miles to the St. Helena Picnic Shelter on the right. The trailhead is at the south end of the parking lot, marked with a pink blaze.

SILVER LAKE BREWING PROJECT

Since opening in the small farming town of Perry in 2016, the Silver Lake Brewing Project has emphasized its ties to the local community. The downtown location, a refurbished brick building that formerly housed the *Perry Shopper* free newspaper, sports a giant mural of a sea serpent, the brewery's logo—a reference to the Silver Lake Serpent, a local legend that grew from native Seneca lore into a 19th-century hoax centering around the nearby lake. Inside the welcoming, well-lit tasting room, you'll find locals and "lakers" mingling over a variety of beers. The Standard cream ale, a uniquely American brew, is a modern take on the style popularized in the 1960s by Genesee Beer in nearby Rochester. The brewery hosts frequent live music shows and various other events, including an annual foosball tournament.

LAND MANAGER

NYS Department of Parks, Recreation, and Historic Preservation
1 Letchworth State Park
Castile, NY 14427
(585) 493-3600
www.parks.ny.gov/parks/letchworth
Map: www.parks.ny.gov/documents/parks/LetchworthLetchworthMap.pdf

BREWERY/RESTAURANT

Silver Lake Brewing Project
14 Borden Avenue
Perry, NY 14530
(585) 969-4238
www.silverlakebrewingproject.com
Distance from trailhead: 12.2 miles

WATKINS GLEN STATE PARK

AWE-INSPIRING WATERFALL VIEWS

WATKINS GLEN

▷⋯ STARTING POINT	⋯✗ DESTINATION
WATKINS GLEN STATE PARK VISITOR CENTER	**JACOB'S LADDER**
🍺 BREWERY	🎯 HIKE TYPE
UPSTATE BREWING COMPANY	**MODERATE**
🐾 DOG FRIENDLY	📅 SEASON
NO	**APRIL–OCTOBER**
$ FEES	⏱ DURATION
$10 (FREE WITH EMPIRE PASS)	**1 HOUR 30 MIN.**
⛰ MAP REFERENCE	↦ LENGTH
POSTED AT TRAILHEAD	**2.4 MILES** (LOOP)
🔍 HIGHLIGHTS	〰 ELEVATION GAIN
WATERFALLS	**550 FEET**

COMMON SENSE ALE

AMBER

MALT,
CARAMEL,
APPLE

TOASTY,
HINT OF COFFEE

BITTERNESS	SWEETNESS
1	2

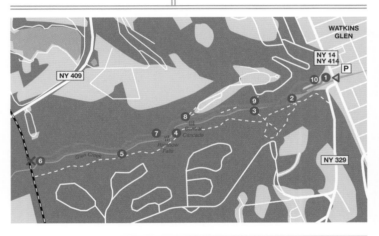

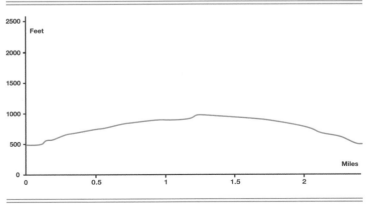

HIKE DESCRIPTION

Brave the crowds—and the stairs—to experience one of the most breathtaking hikes you'll ever take. Then enjoy a pint at the brand-new Upstate Brewing Company tasting room in the charming lakeside town of Watkins Glen.

Falling 400 feet in less than two miles, Glen Creek cuts a narrow ravine between overhanging cliffs on its course to nearby Seneca Lake. The result is a shaded, misty, surreal environment. Passing through it, you'll follow stone staircases as they wind upstream and cross incredible waterfalls on beautiful bridges.

Watkins Glen State Park is situated on the edge of downtown Watkins Glen, a lakeside tourist town known as a mecca of North American auto racing. Directly outside the park entrance, the original start/finish line of the famous road course is marked in checkered-flag paint. Watkins Glen hosted the first postwar auto race in the US. Racing continued for several years on a course that wound through the village on public roads, until an unfortunate fatality and resulting concerns over spectator safety forced the construction of a closed racecourse in 1956.

The hike is not long, but it does gain over 500 feet of elevation in a fairly short distance as the trail climbs from the floor of the gorge to the overlooking rim. In all, you'll climb up more than 800 steps over the course of the hike. Take care throughout, as the rock is often wet and slippery. Owing to the dazzling beauty of the falls, the Gorge Trail sees over a million visitors a year, so plan to visit early in the morning or late in the afternoon, when crowds are a bit thinner. Also, while the rim trails on either side of the gorge are open year-round and allow leashed pets, the Gorge Trail itself is closed from November through May due to ice accumulation and rockfall danger, and dogs are not permitted.

The climbing begins almost immediately upon entering the gorge. You'll ascend a narrow spiral staircase to cross Sentry Bridge, a stone span suspended high above the lowermost of the park's nineteen waterfalls. Making your way upstream, you'll encounter breathtaking views of multiple cascades and plunge pools. An immediate highlight, barely a quarter-mile up the trail, is Cavern Cascade. The trail crosses behind this 50-foot flume and enters Spiral Tunnel, where you'll climb a spiral staircase that ascends inside a cave. After you've passed between the towering walls of Glen Cathedral, you'll come to a stone

bridge that crosses over Central Cascade, which, at 60 feet, is the tallest waterfall in the park. Minutes later, you'll reach the iconic Rainbow Falls, where a misty cascade plunges into an emerald pool framed by narrow cliffs and stone stairs.

After passing behind Rainbow Falls, you'll continue to ascend through Spiral Gorge. You'll pass Mile Point Bridge before reaching the final climb, a 180-step staircase known as Jacob's Ladder. At the top, you'll reach the upper entrance to the park. A shuttle connects to the main entrance during the summer months, so you can ride the bus back to the start if you wish; you can also start your hike by taking the shuttle here and walking down the Gorge Trail if you don't want to climb all those stairs! The top of Jacob's Ladder marks the start of the Indian Trail (also called the North Rim Trail). This mile-long stretch makes a nice downhill return route to the start (with good footing along the rim), though views of the gorge itself are limited.

TURN-BY-TURN DIRECTIONS

1. From the visitor center, head west, following signs for the Gorge Trail.
2. At 0.2 miles, cross the stone Sentry Bridge, the first of several creek crossings.
3. At 0.4 miles, a side trail off of the Indian Trail joins from the right. Continue straight on the Gorge Trail.
4. At 0.6 miles, Lover's Lane joins from the right. Continue on the Gorge Trail.
5. At 0.8 miles, reach Rainbow Falls. Continue on the Gorge Trail.
6. At 1.3 miles, reach the end of the Gorge Trail and climb the staircase. At the top of the stairs, turn right onto the Indian Trail/North Rim Trail.
7. At 1.7 miles, pass the side trail to Mile Point Bridge on the right and continue on the North Rim Trail.
8. At 1.9 miles, the trail forks and a sign on the left indicates an exit from the park. Bear right and continue downhill on the North Rim Trail.
9. At 2.1 miles, reach a large five-way intersection with a suspension bridge on the right. Pass the bridge and head straight/downhill, following signs for the Indian Trail/Gorge Trail/Waterfalls.
10. At 2.3 miles, begin descending a long staircase that bends gradually to the right and terminates just west of the trailhead.

FIND THE TRAILHEAD

From I-86, take Exit 54 toward NY-13 North/Ithaca and continue on NY-13 North for 0.9 miles. At the traffic circle, take the third exit onto East Franklin Street and follow it for 0.8 miles. Make a slight right onto North Main Street and proceed for 0.4 miles, where Main Street becomes Watkins Road. Continue for 8.8 miles, until Watkins Road becomes NY-14. Continue straight on NY-14 North for another 6.9 miles. Pass the large sign for Watkins Glen State Park on the left, turn left at the traffic light onto Pine Street and then make an immediate left to enter the parking lot for the park. The visitor center, gift shop, café, and trailhead are located at the south end of the parking lot.

UPSTATE BREWING COMPANY

The brand-new taproom, just steps from the southern shore of Seneca Lake, is the second location set up by the Elmira-based Upstate Brewing Company. Founder Mark Neumann hopes word will spread about this well-loved brand among the many tourists who flock to the area and that this will complement the statewide distribution that has boosted the brewery's reputation since its founding in 2011. The flagship Common Sense is a revival of the Kentucky Common Ale, a dark, malty ale native to Louisville that all but vanished after Prohibition. The taproom is a long, rectangular space with large garage doors that open invitingly onto outdoor courtyards.

LAND MANAGER

NYS Department of Parks, Recreation, and Historic Preservation
1009 North Franklin Street
Watkins Glen, NY 14891
(607) 535-4511
www.parks.ny.gov/parks/142/
Map: www.parks.ny.gov/documents/parks/WatkinsGlenWatkinsGlenTrail-Map.pdf

BREWERY/RESTAURANT

Upstate Brewing Company
17 North Franklin Street
Watkins Glen, NY 14891
(607) 742-2750
www.upstatebrewing.com
Distance from trailhead: 0.5 miles

BUTTERMILK FALLS

CLIMB THROUGH ONE OF ITHACA'S ICONIC GORGES

ITHACA

▷··· STARTING POINT	···✕ DESTINATION
BUTTERMILK FALLS STATE PARK OFFICE	**LAKE TREMAN**
🍺 BREWERY	卍 HIKE TYPE
ITHACA BEER COMPANY	**MODERATE**
🐾 DOG FRIENDLY	📅 SEASON
YES (LEASH REQUIRED)	**APRIL–NOVEMBER**
$ FEES	⏱ DURATION
$9 (FREE WITH EMPIRE PASS)	**2 HOURS**
⛰ MAP REFERENCE	↦ LENGTH
BUTTERMILK FALLS TRAIL MAP	**4.6 MILES** (LOOP)
👁 HIGHLIGHTS	〜 ELEVATION GAIN
WATERFALLS, LAKE, MARSH, DAM	**968 FEET**

7.2 %
ALCOHOL
CONTENT

FLOWER POWER
IPA

 HAZY YELLOW

 TROPICAL

FRUITY,
STRONG HOPS

BITTERNESS SWEETNESS

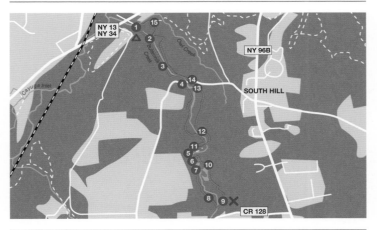

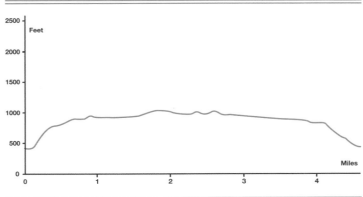

HIKE DESCRIPTION

Climb the stairs alongside a cascading waterfall though one of Ithaca's stunning and iconic gorges. Then visit Ithaca Beer Company for farm-to-table dining and a taste of the legendary Flower Power IPA.

Spend any time near the Finger Lakes and you'll see the slogan on everything from T-shirts to bumper stickers: "ITHACA IS GORGES." The retreat of the glaciers 10,000 years ago carved deep fissures into the rocks surrounding the Finger Lakes, marking the region with stunning waterfalls. Several of these gorges pass right through Ithaca itself. On the eastern side of town, Cornell University's campus is bisected by Cascadilla Gorge and the twin drops of Triphammer Falls and Ithaca Falls. On South Hill, Ithaca College is bordered by Six Mile Creek and the upper reaches of Buttermilk Creek. The water from all of these gorges runs through Ithaca into Cayuga Lake, which, at 39 miles, is the longest of the eleven Finger Lakes.

Buttermilk Falls State Park is one of several parks in the Ithaca area and provides an excellent opportunity to experience the gorges up close. At the entrance to the park, the bottom of Buttermilk Falls empties into a large swimming area that is open to patrons in the summer and is the perfect way to cool off after a day of exploring. You'll begin the hike by ascending the Gorge Trail along the southern side of the falls, utilizing a series of stone staircases. The fabulous views will help to make up for the fact that you're climbing 555 stairs and over 600 vertical feet in just under a mile!

Once you reach the top of the stairs, the most difficult work is done. From here, the trail undulates up and then around Lake Treman, a marshy area formed by an old stone dam across Buttermilk Creek. This section of the park is more secluded, and you're likely to spot cranes and other waterfowl in the area. Complete your circumnavigation of the lake by following the Lake Treman Trail right over the top of the dam. You'll return to the trailhead and the swimming area via the Rim Trail, which parallels the Gorge Trail on the northern side of the falls (alas, with limited views). The Gorge Trail is closed in winter, but the remainder of the trails on this hike are open year-round.

TURN-BY-TURN DIRECTIONS

1. Starting from the park office at the base of the parking lot, head south across a footbridge, keeping the falls and the swimming area on the left. After crossing the bridge, make an immediate left onto the Gorge Trail and begin climbing the stairs.

2. At 0.2 miles, pass a small overlook with a view of the falls on the left.

3. At 0.7 miles, pass a lean-to on the right and a stone footbridge crossing the gorge on the left. Continue straight on the Gorge Trail.

4. At 1.0 miles, reach the top of the stairs at West King Road. Cross the road and continue straight on the red-blazed Bear Trail.

5. At 1.7 miles, emerge into a small clearing with a road directly ahead. Bear right onto a small unmarked grassy path.

6. At 1.8 miles, join the paved Upper Buttermilk Falls Park Road and bear right, following the road southwest toward a small parking lot and restrooms. Cross the parking area, keeping the restrooms on the right, and continue south, following signs indicating "Trail Around Lake".

7. At 1.9 miles, pass an intersection with a white-blazed trail on the left and continue straight, following signs toward Lake Treman.

8. At 2.2 miles, the trail forks. Bear left, following the white-blazed Lake Treman Trail.

9. At 2.4 miles, cross a stone footbridge at the far end of the lake. Bear left, then make another immediate left onto a wide gravel path marked with white blazes.

10. At 2.6 miles, climb a steep wooden staircase, continuing to follow the Lake Treman Trail.

11. At 3.0 miles, the trail forks. Bear left, continuing to follow the Lake Treman Trail. Descend to the lake and cross the stone walkway over the top of the dam. Climb and descend a stone staircase, then cross a short footbridge to complete the loop around the lake. Turn right to return to the upper parking lot.

12. At 3.2 miles, cross the parking lot and bear right, following Upper Buttermilk Falls Park Road.

13. At 3.9 miles, pass through another parking lot with restrooms and a camping area, continuing straight on the road.

14. At 4.0 miles, cross West King Road and continue straight on the red-blazed Rim Trail. The trail immediately forks; bear left and downhill.

15. At 4.4 miles, bear left, following signs for the Rim Trail back to the trailhead.

FIND THE TRAILHEAD

Ithaca is proudly "centrally isolated" and is a solid drive from any major highways. From downtown Ithaca, head west on NY-13 South/NY-96 South for 1.5 miles. The entrance to Buttermilk Falls State Park will be on your left. The main parking area is located just beyond the trailhead at the main office. Restrooms are available on the right as you enter the parking lot.

ITHACA BEER COMPANY

Founded in 1998 by Cornell grad Dan Mitchell, Ithaca Beer Company has grown steadily from a local secret to a regional powerhouse with distribution throughout the East Coast. In 2004, brewer Jeff O'Neill put the brewery on the map with Flower Power, one of the first beers to give the quintessential West Coast IPA an East Coast twist. It was named one of the "25 Most Important American Craft Beers Ever Brewed" by *Food and Wine* magazine in 2018. The main brewery and taproom, opened in 2012, feature a large outdoor seating area (dogs are not allowed) and a farm-to-table restaurant that features ingredients from the brewery's own working farm and other local growers.

LAND MANAGER

NYS Department of Parks, Recreation, and Historic Preservation
112 East Buttermilk Falls Road
Ithaca, NY 14850
(607) 273-5761
www.parks.ny.gov/parks/151/getting-there.aspx
Map: www.parks.ny.gov/documents/parks/ButtermilkFallsTrailMap.pdf

BREWERY/RESTAURANT

Ithaca Beer Company
122 Ithaca Beer Road
Ithaca, NY 14850
(607) 273-0766
www.ithacabeer.com
Distance from trailhead: 0.8 miles

TAUGHANNOCK FALLS

AN EASY STROLL TO ONE OF THE STATE'S TALLEST WATERFALLS

TRUMANSBURG

▷··· STARTING POINT	···✕ DESTINATION
GORGE TRAIL TRAILHEAD PARKING AREA	**TAUGHANNOCK FALLS**
🍺 BREWERY	🗺 HIKE TYPE
LIQUID STATE BREWING COMPANY	**EASY** 🚶
🐾 DOG FRIENDLY	📅 SEASON
YES (LEASH REQUIRED)	**YEAR-ROUND**
$ FEES	🕐 DURATION
$9 (FREE WITH EMPIRE PASS)	**45 MINUTES**
⌂ MAP REFERENCE	↦ LENGTH
POSTED AT TRAILHEAD	**2.0 MILES** (ROUND-TRIP)
🔍 HIGHLIGHTS	〜 ELEVATION GAIN
WATERFALL	**285 FEET**

6.1%
ALCOHOL CONTENT

DAYPACK SAISON

 CLEAR YELLOW

FRUITY

LEMON,
PEPPER

BITTERNESS

SWEETNESS

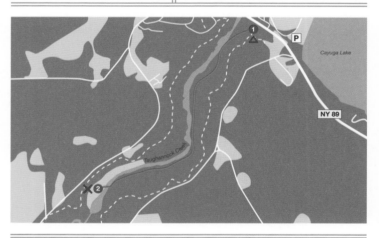

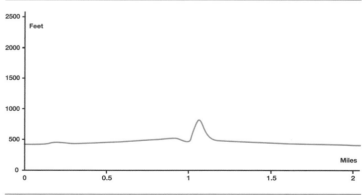

HIKE DESCRIPTION

Take a relaxing stroll through one of the Finger Lakes' many gorges to the base of the tallest waterfall in New York. Then sample the wide variety of beers on tap at Liquid State Brewing Company in the heart of downtown Ithaca.

When we think of waterfalls in New York, what comes to mind? The most famous of the Empire State's two thousand waterfalls is most certainly Niagara Falls, but the tallest single-drop waterfall in New York—reportedly the tallest uninterrupted waterfall in the eastern US—is actually Taughannock Falls. More than half a million visitors travel to the western shores of Cayuga Lake annually to hike the trails through and around the gorge, and to swim in and boat on the longest of the Finger Lakes.

This hike takes you through an area with a rich Native American history. The land was once home to the Cayuga Nation, one of the six tribes that comprised the Iroquois confederacy. The name "Taughannock" has been variously translated as "the great fall in the woods" and "the crevice which rises to the tops of the trees." Some sources note the similarity of the name to the Delaware word for "chief"; one (possibly apocryphal) story claims that the body of a Delaware chief defeated in battle was thrown over the falls, lending the cascade its name.

There are two hiking routes that allow you to experience the majesty of the falls. You can loop around the falls by using the North Rim and South Rim trails. This three-mile route features steep climbs and descents over a series of stone steps as the trail ascends to a height

nearly 200 feet above the top of the waterfall, yielding spectacular views. A 19th-century hotel once stood on the main overlook. Visitors reached the hotel via train (the Black Diamond Trail on the west end of the park follows an old railway bed that once connected nearby Ithaca to far-flung Buffalo, Niagara Falls, and New York City) or by steamboat and stagecoach.

Unfortunately, the rim trails are closed throughout the winter. The easier (and year-round) option is to take the Gorge Trail, which parallels Taughannock Creek for a mile, to the large pool at the base of the falls. This wide, gravel-lined trail is mostly flat and very easy to follow as it tracks the southern bank of the wide creek. On warm summer days, many visitors take the opportunity to wade in the shallow waters. You'll pass through stands of sugar maples and birch trees, which thrive in the dark, moist environment on the canyon floor and contrast beautifully with the red cedars that cling to the south-facing rock walls above. The microclimates on the North and South Rims vary greatly due to their relative exposure to sunlight, so exploring different areas of the park will reveal significant differences in flora.

The Gorge Trail ends at the base of the falls, where you can fully appreciate the 215-foot drop. The waterfall has carved a deep canyon, and the cliffs on either side tower nearly 400 feet overhead. These rock walls are home to numerous birds of prey, including peregrine falcons, which recently returned to the area after a long absence. Spring is a wonderful time to visit, as the snowmelt places the full power of the falls on display.

TURN-BY-TURN DIRECTIONS

1. From the trailhead, head southwest on the Gorge Trail.
2. At 1.0 miles, cross over Taughannock Creek on a wooden footbridge and reach an observation platform at the end of the trail. Retrace your steps to return to the parking area.

FIND THE TRAILHEAD

From downtown Ithaca, take Buffalo Street west to NY-89. Turn right on NY-89 North and follow it for 9.0 miles. The parking lot for the trailhead will be on the left. There are larger parking areas on the right side of the road that provide access to the swimming beach, picnic areas, and boat launch; you can park there and walk to the trailhead if the smaller lot is full.

LIQUID STATE BREWING COMPANY

Visitors to Liquid State's downtown Ithaca digs will be impressed by the variety of beer on offer. There's something for everyone in the brewery's twenty taps, which feature German and Belgian brews, IPAs, porters, stouts, and sours, as well as hard seltzer, kombucha, and local wines and ciders. The expansive beer hall opens onto a view of the brewhouse and fermentation room, with additional outdoor seating available in warmer months. Silo Food Truck, parked permanently outside, serves up fried chicken, mac and cheese, and other homestyle favorites, and the brewery offers wood-fired pizza and soft pretzels.

LAND MANAGER

NYS Department of Parks, Recreation, and Historic Preservation
1738 NY-89
Trumansburg, NY 14886
(607) 387-6739
www.parks.ny.gov/parks/taughannockfalls
Map: www.parks.ny.gov/documents/parks/TaughannockFallsTrailMap.pdf

BREWERY/RESTAURANT

Liquid State Brewing Company
620 West Green Street
Ithaca, NY 14850
(607) 277-0010
www.liquidstatebeer.com
Distance from trailhead: 9.4 miles

ACKNOWLEDGEMENTS

Let's be honest—it's just a guidebook. It's not like we've written *War and Peace*. But any creative undertaking, even on a relatively modest scale, is a team effort. "Success has many fathers, but failure is an orphan." The existence of this book is due in no small part to the help of the following people, to whom we owe many thanks.

Editors Sonia and Ashley Curtis not only took the garbled mess we handed them and turned it into something people would actually want to read, but were amazingly patient answering questions, correcting and re-correcting our mistakes, and basically holding our hands the entire way.

Carey Kish, author of *Beer Hiking New England*, provided indispensable guidance on creating some of the maps and files in this book.

The great New York trail runner Michelle Merlis, who has won *actual* national championships, clued us in to a number of trails and parks in the Capitol Region that we hadn't seen before, including some of our favorites in this book.

The legendary Laura Kline played tour guide and hostess in her adopted hometown of Syracuse, though New Paltz wishes she would just knock it off and move back already.

We have too many hiking and trail-running partners and friends to thank here, and we're really afraid we'll accidentally leave someone out, so to anyone who's accompanied us on our many miles in the Gunks, Cats, and Dacks over the past few years, you know who you are, thank you, let's go for a run.

Jason also wants to thank Jodi for not telling him this was a stupid idea and otherwise being incredibly understanding and supportive, Lexi for being an awesome hiking partner who's never afraid to ask the important questions, and Dylan for being his biggest cheerleader.

Photos by the authors except:
AllTrails: pp. 38, 42, 56, 64, 68, 70, 71, 74, 77, 108, 116, 126, 146, 149, 154, 155, 172, 173, 174, 182, 188, 190, 191, 202, 204, 206, 209, 210, 212, 218, 220, 221
West Kill Brewing: p. 133
Dylan Friedman: p. 8